The History o

Beyond the Pitons

Copyright © 2023 by Shanti Tia Carter and Einar Felix Hansen.

All rights reserved. No part of this publication may be reproduced, stored in a retrieval system, or transmitted, in any form or by any means, electronic, mechanical, photocopying, recording, or otherwise, without the prior written permission of the copyright holder. This book was created with the help of Artificial Intelligence technology.

The contents of this book are intended for entertainment purposes only. While every effort has been made to ensure the accuracy and reliability of the information presented, the author and publisher make no warranties or representations as to the accuracy, completeness, or suitability of the information contained herein. The information presented in this book is not intended as a substitute for professional advice, and readers should consult with qualified professionals in the relevant fields for specific advice.

The Ancient Roots of St. Lucia 6

Indigenous Peoples of St. Lucia 9

Early European Exploration and Colonization 12

Sugar, Slavery, and Plantations 15

The French and British Rivalry 18

Colonial St. Lucia: A Battleground 21

Emancipation and Post-Slavery Era 24

The Rise of the Banana Industry 27

World Wars and St. Lucia's Contribution 30

The Road to Independence 33

Modern Politics and Governance 36

Cultural Diversity and Heritage 39

The Flora and Fauna of St. Lucia 42

Culinary Traditions and Delicacies 45

The Pitons: St. Lucia's Iconic Landmarks 48

Sulphur Springs and Volcanic Wonders 51

Pigeon Island: A Historical Gem 54

Rodney Bay: Tourism Hub 57

Soufrière: A Town Steeped in History 60

Castries: The Capital City 63

Gros Islet: From Fishing Village to Tourist Hotspot 66

Vieux Fort: Gateway to the South 69

Historical Plantations and Estates 72

Folklore and Legends of St. Lucia 74

Religious and Spiritual Traditions 77

Art and Music: The Creative Soul of St. Lucia 80

Education and Literacy 83

Challenges and Triumphs of St. Lucia 86

St. Lucia's Role in the Caribbean Community 89

Tourism's Impact on St. Lucia's Economy 92

Environmental Conservation Efforts 95

Resilience and Recovery: Natural Disasters 98

St. Lucia's Future: Aspirations and Challenges 101

Conclusion 104

The Ancient Roots of St. Lucia

To understand the history of St. Lucia, one must delve into its ancient roots, a tapestry woven with the threads of indigenous cultures and early human settlements. St. Lucia, a small island nestled in the eastern Caribbean Sea, has a history that stretches back millennia, revealing a rich and diverse heritage.

The earliest inhabitants of St. Lucia were the indigenous Amerindian peoples, primarily the Arawaks and later the Caribs. These indigenous cultures arrived on the island around 200-400 AD, long before the arrival of European explorers. They lived in harmony with the lush, tropical environment, relying on fishing, hunting, and agriculture for sustenance. Evidence of their presence can still be found in the form of petroglyphs and artifacts, providing valuable insights into their way of life.

One of the most significant archaeological discoveries on St. Lucia is the rock art at the site of Carambola. These petroglyphs, etched into the island's rocks by ancient hands, depict various motifs, including animals, human figures, and abstract designs. They offer a glimpse into the spiritual and artistic expressions of these early islanders, shedding light on their beliefs and customs.

As centuries passed, St. Lucia became a focal point for trade among neighboring islands and the mainland of South America. The island's strategic location in the Lesser Antilles made it an attractive destination for seafaring communities. The Caribs, known for their seafaring prowess, settled on the island, establishing a presence that would impact its history significantly.

The Caribs were skilled navigators and fierce warriors, often clashing with European explorers who ventured into the Caribbean in the late 15th century. Christopher Columbus, on his fourth voyage to the New World in 1502, sighted St. Lucia, but it wasn't until the mid-16th century that the first European attempts at colonization were made.

The French and the British were the two European powers who vied for control of St. Lucia during the 17th and 18th centuries. The island changed hands several times between these colonial powers, leading to a tumultuous period in its history. The Caribs fiercely resisted European incursions, but by the 18th century, their numbers had dwindled significantly due to conflict, disease, and displacement.

The colonial powers, with their plantations, brought a new era of slavery to St. Lucia. The island's economy became heavily dependent on sugar and other cash crops, leading to the importation of enslaved Africans to work on the plantations. This dark chapter in St. Lucia's history left a lasting legacy that would shape its society and culture for centuries to come.

Despite the challenges of colonization and slavery, the indigenous Amerindian and African influences on the island persisted. The blending of these diverse cultures laid the foundation for St. Lucia's unique heritage, characterized by a vibrant mix of traditions, languages, and customs.

In the midst of colonial struggles, St. Lucia's lush landscape remained a source of both beauty and bounty. The island's volcanic terrain, characterized by dramatic peaks like the iconic Pitons, played a role in shaping its geography and ecology. Dense rainforests, cascading waterfalls, and fertile valleys showcased the natural splendor that would one day attract tourists from around the world.

As we journey through the annals of history, it becomes evident that St. Lucia's ancient roots are intertwined with the rise and fall of civilizations, the resilience of indigenous peoples, and the complexities of colonialism. The echoes of the past reverberate through the island's present-day culture, making it a place where history and heritage continue to shape its destiny.

Indigenous Peoples of St. Lucia

The history of St. Lucia is deeply intertwined with the presence of indigenous peoples who inhabited the island long before the arrival of European colonizers. These early inhabitants, primarily the Arawaks and later the Caribs, played a vital role in shaping the island's culture, society, and landscape.

The Arawaks are believed to have been the first indigenous group to settle on St. Lucia, arriving around 200-400 AD. They were part of the larger Arawakan-speaking peoples who inhabited several islands in the Caribbean. These early St. Lucians were skilled horticulturists, cultivating crops like cassava, sweet potatoes, and yams. They also engaged in fishing and hunting, making the most of the island's abundant natural resources.

Evidence of the Arawak presence on St. Lucia can still be found in the form of archaeological remains, including pottery shards, tools, and ceremonial artifacts. These remnants offer valuable insights into their daily lives, religious practices, and artistic expressions.

The Arawak culture was marked by a strong connection to the natural world. They worshipped deities associated with elements such as water, earth, and the sun. This spiritual bond with the environment is reflected in their art, with motifs featuring animals, plants, and celestial symbols.

Despite their relatively peaceful existence, the Arawaks faced challenges from external forces. As the Caribbean became a hub for trade and travel, the island attracted the attention of more aggressive and warlike peoples, particularly the Caribs.

The Caribs, also known as the Kalinago, arrived in the Caribbean later than the Arawaks, possibly in the 9th century. They were fierce warriors and skilled seafarers, known for their long canoes and raids on neighboring islands. St. Lucia, with its strategic location, became a point of interest for the Caribs, who sought to dominate the island.

The arrival of the Caribs led to conflicts with the Arawaks, who gradually retreated or integrated with the incoming Carib population. The Caribs established a stronghold on St. Lucia, and their presence would leave a lasting mark on the island's history.

Carib society was organized into clans, each with its own chief or leader. They were skilled hunters, fishermen, and agriculturalists, much like their Arawak predecessors. The Caribs were also known for their linguistic prowess, with the Carib language being one of the few surviving indigenous languages in the Caribbean today.

The indigenous peoples of St. Lucia developed intricate social structures and cultural traditions. They crafted tools, utensils, and jewelry from materials like bone, shell, and stone. These artifacts, found in archaeological sites across the island, offer glimpses into their craftsmanship and artistic sensibilities.

As time passed, the arrival of European explorers and colonizers would bring significant changes to the lives of the indigenous peoples of St. Lucia. The struggle for control of the island, the introduction of new diseases, and the forced labor of enslaved Africans would all impact their existence and eventually lead to the decline of their populations.

Yet, the legacy of the Arawaks and Caribs endures in the cultural fabric of St. Lucia. Their contributions to the island's heritage, from language and cuisine to art and spirituality, continue to resonate in modern-day St. Lucian society, serving as a testament to the enduring influence of the indigenous peoples of this remarkable island.

Early European Exploration and Colonization

The early European exploration and colonization of St. Lucia mark a pivotal chapter in the island's history, one defined by the ambitions of European powers, the clash of cultures, and the enduring impact on its people and landscape.

The first recorded European contact with St. Lucia came in the late 15th century when Christopher Columbus, on his fourth voyage to the New World in 1502, sighted the island. However, it was not until the mid-16th century that serious attempts at colonization began.

The island's strategic location in the eastern Caribbean made it an attractive prize for European nations vying for supremacy in the region. France and England emerged as the primary contenders for control of St. Lucia during this period, and their struggles for dominance would shape the island's destiny.

The first European settlement on St. Lucia was established by the French in the early 17th century. They named it "Sainte Alousie" in honor of Saint Lucy, a Christian martyr. The French presence on the island was met with resistance from the indigenous Caribs, who fiercely defended their homeland against the intruders.

Over the decades, St. Lucia changed hands multiple times between the French and the British, reflecting the broader colonial rivalries of the time. The Treaty of Paris in 1763 formally ceded St. Lucia to the British, but the island would return to French control in 1778 during the American Revolutionary War. It wasn't until the Treaty of Paris in 1783 that St. Lucia was definitively ceded to the British, who retained control until 1979.

The colonial period brought profound changes to St. Lucia. The European powers established plantations on the island, primarily for the cultivation of sugar, tobacco, and other cash crops. These plantations relied on enslaved labor, with thousands of Africans forcibly brought to the island to work in brutal conditions. The legacy of slavery left an indelible mark on St. Lucia's society, shaping its demographics, culture, and economy.

The enslaved Africans, along with the indentured laborers from India and other parts of the world, contributed to the island's rich cultural mosaic. Their diverse traditions and languages merged with those of the European colonizers, creating a vibrant and unique blend of cultures that is still evident in St. Lucian society today.

As the plantation economy thrived, St. Lucia became a hub for the Atlantic slave trade, with the bustling port of Soufrière serving as a focal point for the transportation of enslaved Africans to other parts of the Caribbean and the Americas.

The colonial powers also left their architectural and infrastructural imprints on the island. Forts, like Pigeon Island and Fort Charlotte, were constructed to defend against enemy incursions. These historic sites still stand as reminders of the island's turbulent past.

Despite the challenges and hardships faced by the enslaved and indentured populations, they played a crucial role in shaping the island's history. Their struggles for freedom and justice laid the groundwork for the eventual end of slavery and the push for independence.

The early European exploration and colonization of St. Lucia cast a long shadow over the island's history. The enduring legacies of this period, from the architectural remnants of colonial forts to the cultural fusion of its people, continue to shape St. Lucia's identity and provide a window into its complex past.

Sugar, Slavery, and Plantations

The history of St. Lucia during the colonial period is intricately tied to the cultivation of sugar, the institution of slavery, and the sprawling plantations that dominated the island's landscape. This chapter delves into the complex and often brutal dynamics of this era.

Sugar, the "white gold" of the colonial Caribbean, played a central role in the island's economy. The fertile soils and tropical climate of St. Lucia were well-suited for sugar cultivation, and European powers recognized the immense profitability of this commodity. The sugar industry began to flourish in the late 17th century, and by the 18th century, it had become the primary driver of St. Lucia's economy.

The production of sugar was labor-intensive, and European colonizers turned to enslaved Africans to provide the workforce necessary to cultivate and process the crop. The transatlantic slave trade brought thousands of Africans to St. Lucia, where they were subjected to grueling and inhumane conditions on the plantations. The system of slavery stripped individuals of their freedom, dignity, and basic human rights.

Life on the sugar plantations was characterized by harsh labor, brutal punishments, and deplorable living conditions. Enslaved Africans toiled in the fields under the scorching sun, tending to the sugarcane crops. They were subjected to severe exploitation and suffered high mortality rates due to diseases and maltreatment.

The plantation owners, often of European descent, amassed considerable wealth through the labor of enslaved Africans. These wealthy landowners lived lives of luxury, building grand mansions and enjoying the fruits of their labor while the enslaved population endured unimaginable suffering.

The legacy of slavery left deep scars on St. Lucia's society and culture. Families were torn apart, languages were lost, and traditional African customs were suppressed. However, the enslaved population also demonstrated resilience and resistance. They preserved aspects of their African heritage, such as music, dance, and spiritual practices, which would later influence the development of St. Lucian culture.

In the early 19th century, the abolitionist movement gained momentum in Europe and the Americas. Pressure from abolitionists, coupled with the persistent resistance of enslaved Africans, led to the gradual dismantling of the institution of slavery. The British Parliament passed the Abolition of the Slave Trade Act in 1807 and the Slavery Abolition Act in 1833, which abolished slavery in most British colonies, including St. Lucia.

The end of slavery marked a significant turning point in the island's history. The formerly enslaved population faced the challenges of freedom and the need to forge new livelihoods. Many remained on the plantations as paid laborers, while others sought opportunities in other industries, such as agriculture, fishing, and trade.

The sugar industry, which had been the economic backbone of St. Lucia, began to decline in the mid-19th century due to factors such as changes in global sugar markets and the rise of alternative crops. The decline of sugar production had far-reaching economic repercussions on the island, leading to a shift in the agricultural landscape.

Despite the hardships of the sugar and slavery era, the resilience of the people of St. Lucia prevailed. Their collective experiences, both triumphs and tribulations, contributed to the formation of a unique cultural identity that continues to evolve and thrive in the modern era.

The French and British Rivalry

The history of St. Lucia is indelibly marked by the fierce and enduring rivalry between two European colonial powers, France and Britain. Their struggle for dominance over this Caribbean jewel would span centuries and leave an indelible mark on the island's culture, governance, and identity.

St. Lucia's strategic location in the eastern Caribbean made it a coveted prize for both France and Britain. The island changed hands a total of fourteen times between these colonial powers, a testament to their determination to control this valuable piece of the Caribbean puzzle.

The French were the first to establish a settlement on St. Lucia in the early 17th century, naming it "Sainte Alousie" after the Christian martyr Saint Lucy. The island's lush landscapes and fertile soils were well-suited for agriculture, particularly sugar cultivation. French planters established sprawling sugar plantations, and the island soon became a profitable center for sugar production.

The British, however, were not to be outdone. They first laid claim to St. Lucia in 1605 but later withdrew. The island's strategic importance did not escape the British Crown, and they made repeated attempts to establish a foothold. In 1664, the British briefly took control but were soon ousted by the French. This back-and-forth struggle continued for decades.

The Treaty of Paris in 1763 saw St. Lucia formally ceded to the British, marking a significant turning point. However, the island was retaken by the French during the American Revolutionary War in 1778. It wasn't until the Treaty of Paris in 1783 that St. Lucia was definitively returned to British control, which lasted until 1979 when the island gained independence.

The rivalry between the French and British in St. Lucia extended beyond territorial disputes. It influenced the island's governance, legal systems, and culture. Each colonial power sought to impose its language and legal traditions, with the French leaving a lasting impact on St. Lucia's Creole language and civil law system, while the British introduced English as the official language and common law.

The contest for St. Lucia was not limited to military conflicts. Diplomatic negotiations and treaties also played a significant role in determining the island's fate. These negotiations often hinged on larger geopolitical considerations, including the European balance of power and the interests of the colonial empires in the Caribbean.

The rivalry between the French and British on St. Lucia reached its peak during the late 18th century. The island was the stage for several naval battles and land skirmishes, reflecting the broader conflict between these powers during the Revolutionary and Napoleonic Wars. The impact of these conflicts on the island's inhabitants was profound, as St. Lucia's strategic importance made it a focal point of European military engagements.

The colonial period also saw the introduction of enslaved Africans to work on the sugar plantations. Slavery, driven by the economic interests of the colonial powers, left an enduring legacy on St. Lucia, shaping its demographics and culture.

The legacy of the French and British rivalry endures in modern St. Lucia. The island's dual linguistic and legal heritage reflects the centuries of European competition. It also serves as a reminder of the resilience of the St. Lucian people, who navigated the complexities of colonial rule and emerged with a distinct identity and a rich cultural tapestry that draws from both French and British influences.

Colonial St. Lucia: A Battleground

Colonial St. Lucia stands as a testament to the tumultuous history of the Caribbean during the age of European empires. In the struggle for supremacy, the island became a coveted prize, changing hands repeatedly between colonial powers and bearing witness to conflicts that would leave an indelible mark on its landscapes and people.

The contest for St. Lucia between France and Britain in the 17th and 18th centuries transformed the island into a perpetual battleground. Its strategic location in the Lesser Antilles made it a prized possession, serving as a foothold for European colonial ambitions in the Caribbean.

The French were the first to establish a settlement on St. Lucia in the early 17th century, but their presence was met with resistance from the indigenous Caribs. These indigenous peoples fiercely defended their homeland against the intruders, leading to clashes and hostilities that continued for years.

The British, recognizing the island's significance, made multiple attempts to assert control over St. Lucia. The island's fate seemed to oscillate with each European conflict and treaty. In 1664, the British briefly took possession, only to be ousted by the French shortly thereafter. This cycle of colonial struggle continued for decades, with the island changing hands a total of fourteen times between the two powers.

The Treaty of Paris in 1763 marked a turning point, officially ceding St. Lucia to the British. However, the island's control remained uncertain, with the French recapturing it during the American Revolutionary War in 1778. The Treaty of Paris in 1783 returned St. Lucia to British rule, where it would remain until gaining independence in 1979.

The rivalry between the French and British on St. Lucia extended beyond territorial disputes. It influenced the island's governance, legal systems, and culture. Each colonial power sought to impose its language and legal traditions, with the French leaving a lasting impact on St. Lucia's Creole language and civil law system, while the British introduced English as the official language and common law.

The 18th century saw St. Lucia becoming a focal point for naval and military engagements. The island's strategic importance made it a battleground during the Revolutionary and Napoleonic Wars, where both European powers sought to gain control. Land skirmishes and naval battles raged on and around the island, leaving scars on its physical landscape and the memories of its people.

One of the most notable conflicts was the Battle of Saint Lucia in 1778, where the British and French navies clashed in Rodney Bay. This battle, along with others, had a profound impact on the island's history and served as a backdrop to the broader geopolitical struggles of the time.

The legacy of colonial St. Lucia as a battleground is evident in its historic sites and landmarks. Forts like Pigeon Island, Fort Charlotte, and Morne Fortune stand as reminders of the island's military significance. These structures, many of which have been preserved and restored, offer a glimpse into the military history of St.

Lucia and the challenges faced by its inhabitants during this turbulent period.

The struggles of colonial St. Lucia left a lasting imprint on its people and culture. The island's residents navigated the complexities of colonial rule and emerged with a unique identity, drawing from both French and British influences. Today, St. Lucia's rich history as a battleground serves as a testament to the resilience of its people and their ability to shape their destiny amidst the turmoil of colonial rivalry.

Emancipation and Post-Slavery Era

The period of emancipation and the post-slavery era in St. Lucia marked a significant turning point in the island's history, as the shackles of slavery were broken, and the nation embarked on a journey toward freedom, self-determination, and social transformation.

Emancipation in St. Lucia came as a result of legislative changes in the British Empire. The Abolition of the Slave Trade Act of 1807 and the Slavery Abolition Act of 1833 marked the formal end of slavery in most British colonies, including St. Lucia. On August 1, 1834, thousands of enslaved Africans on the island took their first steps toward freedom, as they were officially granted emancipation.

The transition from slavery to freedom was a complex and challenging process. While emancipation brought an end to the legal institution of slavery, it did not immediately erase the legacy of centuries of exploitation and oppression. Formerly enslaved individuals faced the daunting task of forging new lives, identities, and livelihoods in a society still marked by racial and economic inequalities.

One significant development in the post-slavery era was the transition from plantation-based economies to a more diverse agricultural landscape. As sugar production declined in the mid-19th century due to changes in global markets and the rise of alternative crops, many plantations diversified into growing crops like cocoa, coffee, and coconuts. This shift contributed to the diversification of the island's agricultural sector and offered new opportunities for employment and economic development.

The transition from slavery also saw the rise of a newly emerged labor force. The formerly enslaved population, often referred to as "apprentices" during a period of transition, continued to work on the plantations under different labor arrangements. This transition period aimed to gradually introduce them to wage labor and a sense of economic independence.

One significant impact of emancipation was the changing demographic landscape of St. Lucia. The African population, which had been forcibly brought to the island during the era of slavery, became the majority, while the European planter class saw a decline in numbers. This demographic shift had implications for the social and political dynamics of the island.

The post-slavery era also witnessed efforts to provide education and religious instruction to the formerly enslaved population. Missionary organizations, both Catholic and Protestant, established schools and churches, contributing to the spread of literacy and the growth of religious communities.

Despite the promise of freedom, the legacy of slavery continued to cast a shadow over the post-slavery era. Racial tensions, economic disparities, and social inequalities persisted, creating challenges for the newly emancipated population as they sought to carve out a place in a changing society.

In 1871, St. Lucia, along with other British colonies in the Caribbean, underwent a shift in governance with the introduction of Crown Colony rule. This system centralized administrative authority under the British Crown, leading to changes in local governance and representation.

The struggle for social and political rights continued to gain momentum throughout the post-slavery era. In the early 20th century, St. Lucians began to demand greater autonomy and representation in their government. These efforts eventually led to constitutional reforms and the granting of limited self-government in the mid-20th century.

The journey from emancipation to self-determination was marked by challenges, achievements, and the resilience of the St. Lucian people. The legacy of this era continues to shape the island's identity, culture, and commitment to the principles of freedom and equality. The post-slavery era in St. Lucia is a testament to the enduring spirit of a nation determined to shape its own destiny in the face of historical injustices.

The Rise of the Banana Industry

The late 19th and early 20th centuries witnessed a remarkable transformation in the economic landscape of St. Lucia with the emergence of the banana industry as a dominant force. This chapter explores how this once-small-scale agricultural endeavor burgeoned into a key pillar of the island's economy.

Bananas, a tropical fruit, had been cultivated in St. Lucia since the early colonial period. However, it was not until the late 19th century that the banana industry experienced exponential growth. Several factors converged to facilitate this transition, reshaping the island's agricultural and economic dynamics.

One pivotal development was the construction of infrastructure, such as roads and railways, which improved transportation and connectivity across the island. These improvements made it possible for farmers to transport their produce more efficiently from the fertile interior regions to coastal ports for export.

Another critical factor in the rise of the banana industry was the introduction of steamships, which revolutionized global trade. Steamships provided a faster and more reliable means of transporting perishable goods like bananas to international markets. This technological advancement opened up new opportunities for St. Lucian banana growers to access overseas consumers.

The efforts of agricultural pioneers and entrepreneurs were instrumental in promoting banana cultivation. Early visionaries recognized the potential of this tropical fruit and began to experiment with different banana varieties and farming techniques. Their efforts laid the foundation for the industry's expansion.

The role of United Fruit Company, a powerful American corporation, cannot be overstated in the development of St. Lucia's banana industry. The company played a dominant role in organizing and modernizing banana production, providing access to global markets, and investing in the construction of infrastructure on the island.

Under the guidance of United Fruit Company, banana plantations proliferated across St. Lucia, transforming vast tracts of land into banana fields. These plantations were characterized by large-scale, monoculture farming methods, which maximized efficiency and productivity but also posed environmental challenges.

Labor was a critical component of the banana industry's success. The demand for a reliable workforce led to increased migration from other Caribbean islands. St. Lucia saw an influx of laborers from neighboring countries, primarily Saint Vincent and the Grenadines, who came to work on the banana plantations. This migration would shape the island's demographic makeup and contribute to its cultural diversity.

The expansion of the banana industry also brought changes to the social and economic fabric of St. Lucia. It provided employment opportunities for many, albeit often under challenging conditions. Workers' rights and labor conditions became topics of concern, leading to labor movements and calls for improved working conditions and wages.

Banana production in St. Lucia faced its fair share of challenges. Disease outbreaks, such as Panama disease and Black Sigatoka, threatened banana crops and required continuous efforts to develop disease-resistant varieties and implement pest control measures.

The economic dependence on bananas exposed St. Lucia to fluctuations in global banana markets. The preferential trade agreements that Caribbean banana-producing nations had with European markets, known as the "banana wars," created uncertainty and instability for the industry.

Despite these challenges, the banana industry remained a vital component of St. Lucia's economy throughout the 20th century. Bananas became a symbol of the island, and the industry played a significant role in shaping its identity and providing livelihoods for thousands of St. Lucians.

As St. Lucia moved into the 21st century, efforts were made to diversify the economy and reduce dependence on bananas. Tourism, agriculture, and other sectors received increased attention, reflecting the need for a more balanced and resilient economy.

The rise of the banana industry in St. Lucia is a story of innovation, investment, and the pursuit of economic opportunity. It transformed the island's agricultural landscape, impacted its society and culture, and served as a reminder of the island's ability to adapt and thrive in the face of economic challenges and opportunities.

World Wars and St. Lucia's Contribution

The tumultuous 20th century witnessed two devastating world wars that reshaped the geopolitical landscape and had far-reaching effects on nations around the globe. St. Lucia, though a small island in the Caribbean, made significant contributions to these global conflicts, both in terms of manpower and resources.

World War I, which raged from 1914 to 1918, marked the first major global conflict of the 20th century. Although St. Lucia was a British colony at the time, its people, like many across the British Empire, felt a strong sense of duty to support the war effort. Thousands of St. Lucian men volunteered to serve in the British armed forces, including the Army and the Royal Navy.

St. Lucian soldiers played critical roles in various theaters of the war. They were deployed to Europe, the Middle East, and Africa, contributing their skills, bravery, and resilience to the Allied forces. Many St. Lucians were involved in frontline combat, while others served in vital support roles, including as medics, engineers, and laborers.

The impact of World War I was deeply felt on the island. The war had economic repercussions, disrupting global trade and affecting St. Lucia's agricultural exports, including bananas. The returning veterans faced challenges as they reintegrated into civilian life, and the island saw the emergence of veterans' organizations aimed at supporting these individuals.

World War II, which spanned from 1939 to 1945, brought a new wave of global conflict. St. Lucia once again rallied to support the Allied forces, with a significant number of its citizens volunteering for military service. This time, the war's effects were more immediate and visible on the island.

The construction of military bases and installations became a focal point of St. Lucia's contribution to World War II. The island's strategic location in the Caribbean made it an important outpost for the Allied forces. Military infrastructure, such as airstrips, naval bases, and defense fortifications, was established to safeguard the region from Axis threats.

One notable development during World War II was the construction of what is now George F. L. Charles Airport, originally known as Beane Field. This airfield played a vital role in facilitating the movement of military aircraft and personnel throughout the Caribbean theater.

St. Lucia's geographic position also made it a key player in the Battle of the Caribbean, where the Allies sought to protect vital sea routes and prevent Axis naval incursions in the region. The island became a hub for naval operations, with British, American, and Canadian naval vessels using St. Lucia as a base for anti-submarine patrols and convoy protection.

In addition to its military contributions, St. Lucia faced the economic and social consequences of the war. The disruption of global trade once again impacted the island's banana industry and led to increased efforts to diversify the economy.

The end of World War II brought about significant changes in St. Lucia and the wider Caribbean. The returning veterans, often referred to as the "Greatest Generation," played a role in shaping the post-war era. The experiences of these veterans, along with the impact of the war on the island's infrastructure and economy, influenced the trajectory of St. Lucia's development in the years that followed.

The contributions of St. Lucia to both World War I and World War II, though small in comparison to larger nations, underscore the island's commitment to global peace and security. The island's role in supporting the Allied forces, its strategic significance in the Caribbean, and the sacrifices made by its people during these conflicts are a testament to the resilience and dedication of St. Lucians in the face of world-changing events.

The Road to Independence

The journey toward independence for St. Lucia, like many other nations in the Caribbean, was a complex and transformative process that spanned several decades. The desire for self-determination, sovereignty, and the ability to shape their own destiny guided the people of St. Lucia along this path to independence.

The post-World War II era brought significant changes to the global political landscape, and the winds of change reached the shores of St. Lucia. The impact of the war, coupled with shifts in international geopolitics, played a role in the decolonization process across the British Empire.

In the years following World War II, there was a growing sense of nationalism and a desire for greater autonomy among St. Lucians. The experiences of St. Lucian veterans who had served in the war contributed to a sense of self-confidence and the belief that the time had come for the island to chart its own course.

In 1951, St. Lucia saw the establishment of an Executive Council with limited self-government. This marked an important step toward greater autonomy. The Executive Council consisted of both elected and appointed members, offering a glimpse of the island's evolving political landscape.

The call for constitutional reform and increased representation gained momentum. Political parties emerged, with the St. Lucia Labour Party (SLP) and the

People's Progressive Party (PPP) being prominent voices advocating for change. Elections in 1954 and 1957 resulted in a more representative government, with the SLP under the leadership of Sir George Charles forming the majority.

The attainment of universal adult suffrage in 1951 was a significant milestone, granting the right to vote to all adults regardless of gender, property, or other qualifications. This marked a step toward a more inclusive and democratic political system.

The pace of constitutional reform accelerated, leading to the establishment of a ministerial system in 1956. Under this system, executive authority was transferred from the British-appointed governor to a locally elected ministerial government. Sir George Charles became the island's first Chief Minister, a significant moment in the island's political history.

As the push for greater self-determination continued, St. Lucia was granted Associated Statehood with the United Kingdom in 1967. This status provided the island with a significant degree of autonomy in internal and external affairs while maintaining a constitutional link with Britain.

The path to full independence was not without challenges and debates. Issues such as economic stability, the role of the British Crown, and the structure of the future government were subjects of discussion and negotiation.

On February 22, 1979, St. Lucia officially became an independent nation, marking the culmination of years of effort and negotiation. The island celebrated its newfound sovereignty with a flag-raising ceremony, cultural performances, and a sense of pride in achieving self-rule.

Independence brought with it the responsibility of self-governance, and St. Lucia embarked on a journey to shape its own destiny. The island continued to face economic challenges, but the determination of its people, coupled with the beauty of its landscapes and the richness of its culture, positioned St. Lucia as a nation with tremendous potential.

The road to independence was a transformative journey that saw the people of St. Lucia embrace the principles of democracy, self-determination, and nationhood. It marked the end of an era of colonial rule and the beginning of a new chapter in the island's history as an independent and sovereign nation in the Caribbean.

Modern Politics and Governance

The era of modern politics and governance in St. Lucia has been characterized by a dynamic political landscape, economic challenges, and a commitment to democratic principles. As the nation embraced its independence, it faced the task of building a stable and prosperous society while navigating the complexities of global politics and economic fluctuations.

Following independence in 1979, St. Lucia adopted a democratic system of government with regular elections and a parliamentary structure. The first Prime Minister of independent St. Lucia was Sir John Compton, a key figure in the nation's early post-independence politics. His leadership played a crucial role in shaping the direction of the newly independent nation.

The political landscape in St. Lucia has been marked by the presence of multiple political parties, each with its own vision and platform. The St. Lucia Labour Party (SLP) and the United Workers Party (UWP) have been the dominant political forces, engaging in competitive elections that reflect the democratic spirit of the nation.

One significant aspect of modern politics in St. Lucia has been the evolution of coalition governments. While the UWP and SLP have taken turns in holding power, coalition arrangements and alliances with smaller parties have occasionally played a role in government formation. These shifts in political dynamics have led to a degree of political stability and continuity.

Economic challenges have been a consistent feature of modern governance in St. Lucia. The island's small size and vulnerability to external economic factors have made it susceptible to fluctuations in global markets. The banana industry, once a pillar of the economy, faced difficulties due to changes in trade preferences and the impact of diseases on banana crops.

To address these economic challenges and promote diversification, St. Lucia has made efforts to develop other sectors, including tourism, agriculture, and services. Tourism, in particular, has grown significantly, with the island attracting visitors from around the world to its stunning beaches, lush landscapes, and vibrant culture.

The tourism sector's growth has led to infrastructure development, including the expansion and modernization of airports and the construction of hotels and resorts. The industry has also created employment opportunities for many St. Lucians, contributing to the nation's economy.

Education and healthcare have been areas of focus in modern governance. Investments in education have led to improved access to primary and secondary education, and St. Lucian students have pursued higher education both locally and abroad. The nation's healthcare system has seen advancements, with improvements in healthcare facilities, access to medical services, and public health programs.

Efforts to address social issues, including poverty, unemployment, and inequality, have been ongoing in St. Lucia. Government initiatives and programs aimed at improving the well-being of citizens have sought to create a more equitable society.

Modern politics in St. Lucia has also seen the nation engage in international diplomacy and regional cooperation. St. Lucia is a member of regional organizations such as the Caribbean Community (CARICOM) and the Organisation of Eastern Caribbean States (OECS), which promote economic integration and cooperation among member states.

The nation has also faced global challenges, including climate change and natural disasters. St. Lucia, like other Caribbean nations, is vulnerable to hurricanes and rising sea levels. Efforts to address climate change and build resilience have been central to the government's agenda.

In the realm of governance, St. Lucia has upheld democratic principles, including free and fair elections, freedom of speech, and a vibrant civil society. The judiciary operates independently, ensuring the rule of law and protection of citizens' rights.

As St. Lucia moves further into the 21st century, it continues to face the complexities of modern governance. The nation's leaders and citizens are confronted with the task of addressing economic challenges, safeguarding the environment, and ensuring the well-being of its people, all within the framework of a democratic society committed to the principles of self-determination and sovereignty.

Cultural Diversity and Heritage

St. Lucia, a vibrant Caribbean nation, is a melting pot of cultures and heritage, with a rich tapestry woven from the threads of its history, indigenous roots, colonial influences, and the contributions of its diverse population. This chapter delves into the cultural diversity and heritage that have shaped the identity of the island and its people.

The Indigenous Peoples: St. Lucia's cultural heritage begins with its indigenous inhabitants, the Arawak and Carib peoples. These indigenous communities left an indelible mark on the island's traditions, including the use of cassava, a staple crop, and their distinctive pottery and art forms. Their presence is a testament to the island's ancient roots.

African Influence: The period of African enslavement during the colonial era brought African cultures to St. Lucia. Enslaved Africans brought with them a rich heritage of music, dance, and storytelling. Elements of African spirituality and religion also found their way into the island's cultural fabric, creating a syncretic blend of beliefs.

European Colonial Legacy: The colonial history of St. Lucia left lasting imprints on its culture. French and British colonial rule significantly influenced the island's language, legal systems, and architecture. The legacy of the French is particularly evident in the Creole language and civil law system, while the British introduced English as the official language and common law.

Music and Dance: St. Lucia's music and dance are vibrant expressions of its culture. Traditional rhythms like the quadrille and the juba dance showcase the island's African and European influences. Calypso and soca music have also become integral to St. Lucian culture, with the island producing talented musicians and artists who have gained international recognition.

Carnival: St. Lucia's Carnival is a colorful and exuberant celebration of its cultural diversity. Rooted in African and European traditions, Carnival features vibrant costumes, parades, and music. The festivities, including the crowning of a Carnival Queen and the steelpan competitions, draw locals and visitors alike.

Cuisine: St. Lucian cuisine is a tantalizing fusion of flavors. The use of fresh, locally sourced ingredients like coconut, fish, and tropical fruits results in dishes that are both delicious and distinctive. Favorites include green fig and saltfish, callaloo soup, and various seafood dishes. Street food, such as the beloved "bake and shark," offers a taste of authentic St. Lucian flavors.

Religion: Religion plays a significant role in the cultural tapestry of St. Lucia. Christianity, with denominations such as Catholicism, Anglicanism, and various Protestant sects, is widely practiced. Alongside Christianity, traditional and syncretic belief systems, influenced by African and indigenous spirituality, continue to have a presence in the lives of many St. Lucians.

Festivals and Celebrations: St. Lucia's calendar is filled with festivals and celebrations that reflect its diverse cultural heritage. La Rose and La Marguerite are floral festivals that honor Saint Rose de Lima and Saint Margaret, blending African and European traditions. The Feast of St.

Lucia, celebrated on December 13th, is a national holiday marked by parades and festivities.

Language and Literature: St. Lucian literature, often written in English and Creole, reflects the island's complex cultural history. Writers like Derek Walcott, a Nobel laureate in literature, have gained international acclaim for their contributions to Caribbean literature. Their works explore themes of identity, history, and the human condition.

Art and Craft: St. Lucia's artistic expression extends to visual arts and crafts. Local artists create paintings, sculptures, and pottery inspired by the island's natural beauty and cultural heritage. Craftsmen produce intricate baskets, textiles, and jewelry that showcase the craftsmanship of St. Lucians.

Heritage Sites: St. Lucia's cultural heritage is preserved in its historic sites and landmarks. Forts like Pigeon Island, Morne Fortune, and Fort Charlotte offer glimpses into the island's colonial history. The Pitons, a pair of iconic volcanic peaks, are not only natural wonders but also UNESCO World Heritage Sites.

Cultural diversity and heritage are integral to the identity of St. Lucia. The blending of indigenous, African, European, and other influences has created a unique cultural mosaic that continues to evolve, celebrating the island's past while shaping its future. St. Lucia's cultural richness is a source of pride for its people and an invitation for visitors to explore the vibrant tapestry of this Caribbean nation.

The Flora and Fauna of St. Lucia

St. Lucia, nestled in the heart of the Caribbean, boasts a remarkable diversity of flora and fauna, a testament to the island's lush landscapes and unique ecosystems. From its dense rainforests to its pristine coral reefs, St. Lucia's natural world is a treasure trove of biodiversity and ecological wonders.

Flora:

1. Rainforests: St. Lucia is renowned for its lush rainforests, particularly in the interior of the island. These forests are characterized by towering trees, dense undergrowth, and a rich variety of plant species. A highlight is the towering giant fern, which is native to the island.
2. Tropical Fruits: The island is abundant with tropical fruit trees, including banana, coconut, mango, and papaya. These fruits are not only a source of local cuisine but also a key component of St. Lucia's agriculture.
3. Medicinal Plants: St. Lucia's rainforests and plant life are home to a range of medicinal plants, some of which have been traditionally used by the island's inhabitants for generations. Plants like the soursop and neem have known medicinal properties.
4. Orchids: St. Lucia is home to numerous species of orchids, including the rare and vibrant "Black Orchid," which is native to the island. Orchid enthusiasts flock to St. Lucia to witness these exotic blooms.

5. Rainforest Trees: The island's rainforests are dominated by various tree species, such as mahogany, gommier, and gommier blanc. These trees provide habitats for a diverse array of wildlife.
6. Coastal Flora: Along the island's coastlines, you'll find coastal vegetation, including seagrape trees, coconut palms, and mangroves. These plants play a crucial role in stabilizing the shoreline and supporting coastal ecosystems.

Fauna:

1. Birds: St. Lucia is a haven for birdwatchers. The island is home to a variety of bird species, including the Saint Lucia parrot, also known as the "Amazona Versicolor," which is the national bird and an endemic species.
2. Reptiles: Several species of reptiles inhabit St. Lucia, including the iguana, geckos, and a variety of snakes. The island is also home to the critically endangered St. Lucia racer snake, which is the world's rarest snake.
3. Mammals: While mammalian diversity is relatively limited on the island, there are species such as the agouti and the opossum. Marine mammals, including dolphins and whales, can also be spotted in the waters surrounding St. Lucia.
4. Marine Life: St. Lucia's coral reefs and marine environments teem with life. The waters are inhabited by a dazzling array of fish, sea turtles, and other marine creatures. Divers and snorkelers can explore vibrant coral gardens and encounter species like parrotfish and seahorses.
5. Insects and Butterflies: The rainforests of St. Lucia are home to an astonishing variety of insects,

including colorful butterflies like the Zebra Swallowtail and the Julia Butterfly. The island's biodiversity extends to its insect population.
6. Amphibians: Several species of frogs and toads can be found in St. Lucia's rainforests, including the iconic mountain chicken frog. The conservation of these amphibians is a priority due to their vulnerability.
7. Invertebrates: St. Lucia's ecosystems are inhabited by diverse invertebrate species, from land crabs and land snails to various species of butterflies and spiders.

Conservation Efforts:

St. Lucia places a strong emphasis on the conservation of its natural heritage. Protected areas like the Soufrière Marine Management Area and the Edmund Forest Reserve help safeguard critical habitats. Conservation programs aim to protect endangered species and preserve the island's ecological balance.

The rich flora and fauna of St. Lucia are not only a source of pride for its inhabitants but also a draw for eco-tourists and nature enthusiasts from around the world. The island's commitment to preserving its natural wonders ensures that future generations can continue to marvel at the beauty and biodiversity of this Caribbean gem.

Culinary Traditions and Delicacies

St. Lucia's culinary traditions are a delectable blend of flavors and influences, reflecting the island's rich history and diverse cultural heritage. From its Creole dishes to the tantalizing seafood creations, St. Lucia's cuisine is a sensory journey through its past and present.

Creole Cuisine: At the heart of St. Lucian gastronomy lies Creole cuisine, a fusion of African, European, and indigenous influences. Signature dishes like "Green Fig and Saltfish" and "Bouyon" exemplify the island's culinary heritage. Green fig, a type of green banana, is often boiled and served with salted codfish, a staple that echoes the days of African slavery. Bouyon, a hearty soup, features a medley of vegetables, meat, and seasonings.

Coconut: The coconut palm is ubiquitous in St. Lucia and plays a prominent role in its cuisine. Coconut milk and grated coconut are essential ingredients in many dishes, lending a creamy texture and tropical flavor to meals. Coconut oil is widely used for frying and cooking, adding a distinct aroma and taste.

Seafood: As an island nation, St. Lucia boasts an abundance of seafood, and fishing is an integral part of its culture and cuisine. Fresh catches like snapper, grouper, and mahi-mahi are prepared in various ways, from grilled and fried to stewed in flavorful sauces. The island's national dish, "Fish Creole," showcases the bounty of the sea, featuring fish simmered in a spicy tomato-based sauce.

Plantains: Plantains, a starchy banana-like fruit, are a culinary staple in St. Lucia. They are versatile and can be boiled, fried, or roasted. Fried plantains, known as "tostones" or "bakes," are a beloved snack and side dish, offering a sweet and savory contrast.

Callaloo: Callaloo, a leafy green vegetable similar to spinach, is a key ingredient in many St. Lucian dishes. It is used to make a hearty soup of the same name, often cooked with crab or salted pork for added flavor. Callaloo is celebrated not only for its taste but also for its cultural significance.

Piton Beer: St. Lucia's own Piton Beer is a refreshing local brew named after the iconic Piton mountains. It is a popular choice among locals and visitors alike, offering a cool respite from the Caribbean sun.

Spices and Seasonings: St. Lucian cuisine is celebrated for its bold and flavorful seasonings. Aromatic spices like thyme, basil, and scallions infuse dishes with depth and character. The island's famous "green seasoning," a blend of fresh herbs and spices, is used to marinate meats and seafood.

Street Food: St. Lucia's street food scene is a vibrant and flavorful experience. Food vendors and stalls offer an array of mouthwatering treats, including "bakes" filled with saltfish or meat, "roti" wraps, and grilled skewers of succulent chicken or fish. The "shark and bake" is a beloved street food delicacy, featuring deep-fried shark served in a bread roll.

Fruit Juices: St. Lucia's tropical climate yields a bounty of fruits, and fresh fruit juices are a popular and refreshing beverage choice. Exotic fruits like soursop, passion fruit, and guava are transformed into delicious, naturally sweet juices.

Desserts: St. Lucia's sweet tooth is satisfied with delightful desserts like "sweet potato pudding," "cassava pone," and "coconut turnovers." These treats often incorporate local ingredients and traditional flavors.

Rum: St. Lucia is known for its rum production, with distilleries crafting a range of rum varieties. Award-winning rums like "Chairman's Reserve" and "Piton Beer" are enjoyed by locals and celebrated by rum enthusiasts worldwide.

St. Lucia's culinary traditions are a reflection of its history, culture, and natural bounty. Whether savoring the flavors of Creole cuisine or indulging in its seafood delights, exploring the island's culinary landscape is a sensory adventure that invites visitors to savor the tastes and traditions of this Caribbean gem.

The Pitons: St. Lucia's Iconic Landmarks

The twin peaks of the Pitons stand as sentinels, guardians of St. Lucia's breathtaking beauty and natural majesty. Rising dramatically from the Caribbean Sea, these iconic landmarks are a symbol of the island's unique geography and have captivated the imaginations of visitors and locals alike.

The Pitons are two volcanic spires, Gros Piton and Petit Piton, located on the southwestern coast of St. Lucia. These majestic peaks are among the most recognizable and photographed landmarks in the Caribbean. Gros Piton, the taller of the two, soars to an impressive height of 2,619 feet (798 meters), while Petit Piton reaches 2,438 feet (743 meters) above sea level. Their distinctive conical shapes and lush greenery make them a striking sight against the azure backdrop of the Caribbean Sea.

These remarkable formations are the result of ancient volcanic activity that shaped the island of St. Lucia millions of years ago. The Pitons are classified as volcanic plugs or lava domes, formed when magma hardens within a volcano's vent, creating a steep-sided pinnacle. Over time, erosion has sculpted the Pitons into their current iconic forms.

Beyond their geological significance, the Pitons have deep cultural and historical importance to the people of St. Lucia. They are an integral part of the island's identity, serving as a symbol of St. Lucia and its unique character.

The Pitons have been designated as a UNESCO World Heritage Site since 2004, recognizing their natural and cultural significance.

The Pitons are not merely static formations; they are living entities, surrounded by lush rainforests, rich biodiversity, and vibrant marine life. The slopes of these mountains are covered in a variety of vegetation, including tropical rainforest, ferns, and endemic plant species. Hiking trails provide opportunities for adventurers to explore the dense forests and marvel at the flora and fauna that call this area home.

For outdoor enthusiasts, climbing Gros Piton is a challenging and rewarding experience. The ascent takes hikers through diverse ecosystems, from dry forest to cloud forest, offering panoramic views of the surrounding landscapes and the Caribbean Sea. Hiking Petit Piton is more technically demanding and is typically reserved for experienced climbers.

The waters around the Pitons are equally captivating. Snorkeling and diving enthusiasts can explore the vibrant coral reefs and underwater ecosystems, discovering a kaleidoscope of marine life that thrives in these protected waters.

The Pitons are not only natural wonders but also provide a backdrop for the island's vibrant culture and festivities. The annual Piton International Film Festival celebrates film in the heart of this stunning setting, attracting filmmakers and enthusiasts from around the world.

Visitors to St. Lucia can savor the beauty of the Pitons from various vantage points. The town of Soufrière, nestled at the base of these mountains, offers stunning views and access to a range of accommodations, from luxury resorts to charming boutique hotels.

Witnessing the sunset cast a warm glow on the Pitons is a magical experience, and many visitors choose to enjoy this spectacle from the deck of a boat, sailing along the island's western coast.

In the presence of the Pitons, time seems to stand still. These natural wonders, with their imposing grandeur and timeless beauty, continue to inspire awe and reverence. They are more than just geological formations; they are an integral part of St. Lucia's identity and a testament to the island's natural riches. To witness the Pitons is to be in the presence of nature's most magnificent creations, a reminder of the Earth's extraordinary capacity for beauty and wonder.

Sulphur Springs and Volcanic Wonders

Nestled in the heart of the Caribbean, St. Lucia boasts not only pristine beaches and lush rainforests but also a unique geological wonder - the Sulphur Springs and volcanic wonders that define the island's southwest region. These natural phenomena are a testament to the island's volcanic origins and offer visitors a glimpse into the Earth's tumultuous geological history.

Sulphur Springs, often referred to as the "drive-in volcano," is one of St. Lucia's most iconic attractions. Located near the town of Soufrière, this geothermal wonder is the world's only "drive-in" volcano, allowing visitors to get up close and personal with its otherworldly features. As you approach Sulphur Springs, the unmistakable scent of sulfur fills the air, a testament to the volcanic activity below.

The centerpiece of Sulphur Springs is a massive crater with bubbling pools of gray mud and steam rising from various vents. This surreal landscape, characterized by its otherworldly appearance, is a result of ongoing volcanic activity beneath the Earth's surface. The mud baths formed by the sulfur-rich water and mineral deposits are renowned for their purported therapeutic properties. Visitors often immerse themselves in these natural baths, believing in the healing benefits of the mineral-rich waters.

The phenomenon of Sulphur Springs is a testament to the island's volcanic history. St. Lucia is part of the Lesser Antilles volcanic arc, a region where tectonic plates converge, creating the conditions for volcanic activity. Sulphur Springs is essentially a dormant volcano, part of a larger volcanic complex that includes the iconic Pitons.

Aside from Sulphur Springs, St. Lucia is home to other volcanic wonders that intrigue geologists and captivate tourists. The Pitons themselves, Gros Piton and Petit Piton, are volcanic plugs formed by ancient magma. These twin peaks, with their dramatic conical shapes, are not only iconic landmarks but also reminders of the island's geological heritage.

St. Lucia's volcanic legacy has also shaped its coastline, resulting in unique geological formations. The "Diamonds" and "Troumassee" are examples of natural rock formations sculpted by volcanic forces and the erosive power of the sea. The dramatic cliffs and hidden coves along the coast are a testament to the dynamic geological history of the island.

Another volcanic wonder on the island is the Diamond Waterfall and Botanical Gardens, located in the Soufrière Estate. The waterfall's vibrant hues, ranging from yellow to purple, are a result of the mineral-rich waters that flow from the volcanic springs. The nearby botanical gardens showcase a diverse collection of tropical flora, creating a lush oasis amidst the volcanic landscapes.

As visitors explore St. Lucia's volcanic wonders, they gain a deeper appreciation for the Earth's geological forces and the profound impact they have had on the island's landscapes. The juxtaposition of pristine beaches and dense rainforests with these geothermal and volcanic attractions adds to the island's allure, making it a destination that offers both natural beauty and a glimpse into the Earth's inner workings.

In many ways, Sulphur Springs and the volcanic wonders of St. Lucia provide a unique lens through which to view the island's geological past and its ongoing transformation. These attractions invite visitors to marvel at the Earth's ancient processes and, in the case of the Sulphur Springs mud baths, even immerse themselves in the healing and rejuvenating powers of the Earth's geothermal energies. St. Lucia's volcanic wonders are not only geological marvels but also an integral part of the island's cultural and natural heritage.

Pigeon Island: A Historical Gem

Pigeon Island, a small but historically significant islet located off the northwest coast of St. Lucia, stands as a testament to the island's rich and complex history. This tiny treasure has witnessed centuries of human activity, from its use as a strategic military outpost to its role in shaping the course of Caribbean history.

The origins of Pigeon Island date back to the indigenous Arawak and Carib peoples, who inhabited the Caribbean long before the arrival of European explorers. These early inhabitants utilized the island for various purposes, including fishing and as a lookout point for spotting potential threats from the sea.

However, it was during the colonial era that Pigeon Island's historical significance truly began to take shape. In the 1550s, the French established a fortification on the islet, recognizing its strategic location. They named it "Isla de las Palomas," meaning "Island of the Pigeons." This initial fortification, known as Fort Rodney, was a modest structure compared to the formidable fortifications that would later adorn the island.

During the 17th and 18th centuries, Pigeon Island changed hands multiple times between the French and the British, reflecting the broader colonial conflicts in the Caribbean. The British, in particular, recognized the importance of Pigeon Island as a vantage point from which to monitor and defend against potential naval threats.

In the late 18th century, Pigeon Island played a crucial role in the Battle of Saint Lucia, a pivotal conflict during the American Revolutionary War. British forces, under the leadership of Admiral George Rodney, used the island as a base to monitor French naval movements and ultimately emerged victorious in the battle. Rodney's victory secured British control of St. Lucia.

The 18th-century fortifications on Pigeon Island were expanded and reinforced during this period, and today, visitors can explore the remnants of these military structures. Fort Rodney, in particular, is a well-preserved historical site, offering panoramic views of the surrounding waters and mainland St. Lucia.

Pigeon Island's history continued to evolve during the colonial era. It served as a quarantine station for ships arriving in St. Lucia, a crucial measure to prevent the spread of diseases. The island's strategic importance persisted through the 19th century, even as the Caribbean underwent significant political changes.

In 1979, St. Lucia achieved independence from British rule, marking a new chapter in the island's history. Pigeon Island, with its historical significance, was designated a National Park, ensuring the preservation of its cultural and natural heritage. Today, it remains a popular destination for both history enthusiasts and nature lovers.

Visitors to Pigeon Island can explore its historical sites, including the well-preserved Fort Rodney, which houses a museum showcasing artifacts and insights into the island's past. The site also hosts cultural events and festivals, offering a glimpse into the vibrant traditions of St. Lucia.

Pigeon Island's natural beauty is equally captivating. Its beaches, hiking trails, and lush landscapes provide opportunities for outdoor enthusiasts to immerse themselves in the island's natural wonders. The picturesque surroundings make it a popular location for weddings, picnics, and leisurely strolls.

Pigeon Island, with its rich history and breathtaking scenery, embodies the spirit of St. Lucia's past and present. It serves as a reminder of the island's complex colonial history, the struggles for control of the Caribbean, and the enduring legacy of its indigenous peoples. Pigeon Island is not merely an islet; it is a historical gem that invites visitors to explore the layers of history that have shaped the Caribbean's cultural tapestry.

Rodney Bay: Tourism Hub

Rodney Bay, located on the northwestern coast of St. Lucia, stands as a vibrant and bustling tourism hub that has earned its reputation as a Caribbean paradise for visitors from around the world. With its pristine beaches, bustling marina, and an array of accommodations, restaurants, and activities, Rodney Bay has become a magnet for tourists seeking sun, sea, and relaxation.

One of Rodney Bay's primary draws is its stunning beaches. Reduit Beach, in particular, is a crescent-shaped expanse of soft, golden sand that stretches along the bay. Framed by swaying palm trees and the azure waters of the Caribbean Sea, Reduit Beach offers the perfect setting for sunbathing, swimming, and water sports. The calm, clear waters make it an ideal spot for snorkeling and paddleboarding, attracting water enthusiasts of all levels.

Beyond Reduit Beach, Rodney Bay is also home to the lesser-known but equally captivating Pigeon Island Beach. This tranquil stretch of shoreline offers a quieter alternative for those seeking a more secluded beach experience.

The Rodney Bay Marina, with its state-of-the-art facilities, has established itself as a premier destination for yacht enthusiasts. It serves as a hub for both seasoned sailors and those looking to explore the Caribbean by sea. The marina is surrounded by waterfront restaurants, shops, and boutiques, creating a lively atmosphere where visitors can enjoy leisurely strolls along the promenade.

In addition to its natural beauty and marine activities, Rodney Bay offers an abundance of dining options. The Rodney Bay Village, a commercial center near the marina, boasts an eclectic mix of restaurants, from casual eateries serving local cuisine to upscale dining establishments offering international flavors. St. Lucian dishes, including fresh seafood, Creole specialties, and tropical fruit cocktails, are staples of the local culinary scene.

The nightlife in Rodney Bay is equally vibrant. The area comes alive after dark with bars, clubs, and entertainment venues that cater to a diverse range of tastes. Whether you're in the mood for live music, dancing, or simply enjoying a Caribbean cocktail under the stars, Rodney Bay's nightlife scene has something for everyone.

Shopping enthusiasts will find plenty to explore in Rodney Bay. The Baywalk Shopping Mall is a popular retail destination, featuring a mix of international brands, local boutiques, and duty-free shops. Visitors can browse for souvenirs, clothing, jewelry, and more while enjoying the air-conditioned comfort of the mall.

For those interested in exploring beyond the beaches and marina, Rodney Bay offers a range of activities and attractions. The nearby Rodney Bay Nature Trail provides an opportunity to immerse oneself in the island's natural beauty and observe local flora and fauna. Water-based excursions, such as catamaran cruises and deep-sea fishing trips, allow visitors to explore the Caribbean Sea and nearby islands.

Rodney Bay has also become a hotspot for hosting events and festivals. Throughout the year, the bay comes alive with celebrations, from the St. Lucia Jazz Festival to various cultural and sporting events. These festivities showcase the island's rich heritage and offer visitors a chance to immerse themselves in St. Lucian culture.

As a tourism hub, Rodney Bay has evolved to cater to the diverse interests of its visitors, offering a blend of relaxation, adventure, and cultural experiences. Whether you seek tranquil days on the beach, exciting water sports, lively nightlife, or a taste of authentic Caribbean cuisine, Rodney Bay invites you to explore its vibrant offerings and discover the beauty and warmth of St. Lucia.

Soufrière: A Town Steeped in History

Nestled on the southwestern coast of St. Lucia, the town of Soufrière is a captivating blend of historical significance, natural wonders, and cultural charm. As one of the oldest towns on the island, Soufrière carries with it a rich tapestry of stories, from its indigenous roots to its colonial past, and from its volcanic landscapes to its vibrant present.

The name Soufrière itself is indicative of the town's volcanic heritage, as it is derived from the French word for sulfur. The town's backdrop is the stunning Soufrière Volcano, which has played a pivotal role in shaping both the town and the island's history. The Soufrière Volcano is famous for its dormant craters, hot springs, and geothermal activity, making it a must-visit attraction for tourists seeking to explore St. Lucia's natural wonders.

Soufrière's history dates back to the Arawak and Carib peoples, who inhabited the island long before the arrival of European explorers. The town's location by the sea and its proximity to the volcano made it a strategically significant area for the indigenous population, who valued its resources and its position as a trade hub.

European colonization in the 17th century brought Soufrière into the realm of colonial powers, with both the French and the British vying for control of the island. The town's natural harbor, sheltered by the iconic Pitons, made it an attractive location for colonial interests. The British ultimately gained control of St. Lucia, and Soufrière continued to thrive under their rule.

During the 18th century, Soufrière experienced significant development. The Diamond Estate, a historic plantation, was established, and its production of sugarcane and cocoa contributed to the town's economic growth. The Soufrière Botanical Gardens, initially created as a plantation reserve, became a focal point for the cultivation of exotic plants and served as a haven for plant enthusiasts.

One of Soufrière's most renowned historical sites is the Diamond Waterfall, which owes its vibrant colors to the minerals carried by the volcanic waters. Visitors to the waterfall can immerse themselves in both its natural beauty and its historical significance, as it is surrounded by remnants of the colonial past, including the mineral baths that were once enjoyed by the European elite.

The town of Soufrière was also the site of significant events during the American Revolutionary War. It was the site of the Battle of Saint Lucia in 1778, a naval engagement between the British and the French, which resulted in the capture of the island by the French. Soufrière's fortifications and strategic location played a role in the conflict and its outcome.

In the 19th century, Soufrière continued to thrive as a center of economic activity, with the cultivation of sugarcane and cocoa driving its prosperity. Plantations like the Fond Doux Estate, which is still operational today, are living testaments to the town's agricultural heritage.

As St. Lucia transitioned to independence in the 20th century, Soufrière retained its historical and cultural significance. The town and its surrounding area became a hotspot for tourism, drawing visitors with its natural beauty, hot springs, and historical sites. The Soufrière region, with its charming architecture and rich history, remains a focal point for those seeking to explore the island's past and experience its vibrant present.

Today, Soufrière's historical charm is complemented by a lively cultural scene, with local festivals, markets, and cultural events that celebrate St. Lucian traditions. The town's colorful streets, Creole architecture, and friendly residents welcome travelers to explore its unique blend of history, culture, and natural wonders.

As a town steeped in history, Soufrière stands as a testament to the enduring legacy of St. Lucia's past. Its volcanic landscapes, colonial heritage, and vibrant present make it a must-visit destination for those seeking a deeper understanding of the island's rich history and cultural tapestry. Soufrière continues to invite visitors to embark on a journey through time, uncovering the stories and treasures that have shaped this captivating Caribbean town.

Castries: The Capital City

Castries, the vibrant capital city of St. Lucia, is a bustling urban center that serves as the heart of the island nation. With its rich history, diverse culture, and picturesque harbor, Castries embodies the spirit of St. Lucia, a dynamic blend of tradition and modernity.

Founded by the French in 1650, Castries was named after Charles Eugène Gabriel de La Croix, Marquis de Castries, a French naval officer. The town's early development was driven by its strategic location along the western coast, which provided access to the Caribbean Sea and made it a natural choice for a colonial settlement.

The history of Castries is marked by a series of colonial transitions, with the town changing hands multiple times between the French and the British during the 18th and 19th centuries. This colonial legacy is still evident in the town's architecture, with some buildings showcasing Creole and Georgian influences.

One of the most iconic landmarks in Castries is Derek Walcott Square, named after the renowned St. Lucian poet and Nobel laureate. The square is home to the Cathedral Basilica of the Immaculate Conception, an impressive Roman Catholic cathedral that stands as a testament to the island's strong religious heritage.

Castries Harbor, also known as Port Castries, is a bustling port that welcomes cruise ships and cargo vessels. The harbor's activity and its scenic views of the surrounding hills make it a focal point for both commerce and tourism.

Visitors can stroll along the harbor's promenade, which offers a mix of local shops, restaurants, and vendors selling souvenirs and crafts.

The Castries Market, a vibrant and colorful hub of activity, provides a glimpse into the island's culture and commerce. Visitors can explore a wide array of goods, including fresh produce, spices, handcrafted jewelry, and local artwork. The market is a lively place to interact with locals and experience the flavors and traditions of St. Lucia.

Castries is also home to a range of cultural institutions, including the National Library and the Folk Research Centre, which promote the preservation and celebration of St. Lucian culture and history. The city's lively arts scene includes theaters, galleries, and cultural festivals that showcase local talent and creativity.

For those interested in history, Fort Charlotte offers panoramic views of Castries and the surrounding coastline. This well-preserved fortification was built during the British colonial era and serves as a reminder of the town's strategic importance in the past.

The culinary scene in Castries is a feast for the senses, with an array of restaurants offering both traditional St. Lucian dishes and international cuisine. The town's nightlife comes alive with bars, clubs, and live music venues that cater to a diverse range of tastes and preferences.

Castries serves as the seat of government for St. Lucia, with notable institutions such as the House of Parliament and the official residence of the Prime Minister, Vigie House. The city's administrative importance is reflected in its infrastructure, including government buildings, embassies, and diplomatic missions.

As the economic, cultural, and political hub of St. Lucia, Castries embodies the island's dynamic character and multicultural heritage. Its mix of historical landmarks, modern amenities, and natural beauty makes it a destination that offers something for every traveler. Castries, with its captivating blend of tradition and progress, invites visitors to explore the heart and soul of St. Lucia, a nation that cherishes its past while embracing the promise of the future.

Gros Islet: From Fishing Village to Tourist Hotspot

Gros Islet, located in the northern part of St. Lucia, is a remarkable testament to the transformation of a quaint fishing village into a vibrant tourist hotspot. This charming town, known for its stunning beaches, lively atmosphere, and world-famous Friday night street party, has evolved over the years, while still retaining its authentic Caribbean charm.

The origins of Gros Islet date back to the Arawak and Carib indigenous peoples who inhabited the island before the arrival of European colonizers. Like many coastal areas in the Caribbean, the town's location by the sea made it an ideal place for fishing and trade. In the early colonial era, Gros Islet was primarily an agricultural and fishing community, its economy driven by the bounties of the Caribbean Sea.

During the 18th and 19th centuries, as St. Lucia changed hands between the French and the British, Gros Islet's role as a fishing village remained central to its identity. The town's history is intertwined with the broader colonial history of the island, marked by periods of British and French rule and the economic activities that accompanied these transitions.

In the early 20th century, the construction of a causeway connecting Gros Islet to the capital, Castries, marked a significant development for the town. This infrastructure improvement enhanced transportation and accessibility, laying the groundwork for future growth and development.

The transformation of Gros Islet from a fishing village into a tourist hotspot gained momentum in the latter half of the 20th century. The town's beautiful beaches, notably Reduit Beach, attracted visitors seeking sun and sea. The construction of hotels and resorts, such as the Bay Gardens Resort, provided accommodations for tourists, while local businesses and restaurants catered to their needs.

One of Gros Islet's most famous attractions is the Gros Islet Friday Night Street Party. What started as a local tradition has grown into an internationally renowned event. Every Friday night, the streets of Gros Islet come alive with music, dancing, and the tantalizing aroma of local cuisine. It's a celebration of St. Lucian culture and a chance for both locals and visitors to come together in a festive atmosphere.

Gros Islet's proximity to the stunning Rodney Bay and the Rodney Bay Marina further bolstered its appeal to tourists. The marina, a hub for sailing and yachting enthusiasts, has become a focal point for maritime activities in the Caribbean, drawing sailors from around the world.

The town's economic transformation has had a profound impact on its community. The tourism industry has provided job opportunities and improved infrastructure, benefiting both residents and visitors. However, Gros Islet has managed to strike a balance between embracing tourism and preserving its cultural heritage.

As Gros Islet continues to evolve as a tourist destination, its local culture remains vibrant. Visitors can explore the traditional open-air markets, where local vendors sell fresh produce, crafts, and souvenirs. The town's churches and historical landmarks, such as the St. Joseph the Worker Parish Church, provide insight into its rich heritage.

Gros Islet's journey from a fishing village to a thriving tourist hotspot is a testament to its adaptability and resilience. It is a place where the past and present coexist harmoniously, where visitors can experience the warm hospitality of its residents while enjoying the natural beauty and vibrant culture of the Caribbean. Gros Islet has found its place on the global tourism map, offering a unique blend of relaxation, entertainment, and authentic Caribbean experiences to all who venture to its shores.

Vieux Fort: Gateway to the South

Vieux Fort, situated at the southernmost tip of St. Lucia, is often referred to as the "Gateway to the South." This bustling town serves as a pivotal entry point to the island, with its international airport and deep-water harbor, and it has a rich history and vibrant present that make it an essential part of St. Lucia's cultural tapestry.

The town's name, "Vieux Fort," is French for "Old Fort," a reference to the historic fortifications that once stood in the area. Vieux Fort has a history that dates back to the early colonial period when European powers vied for control of the Caribbean. The British and the French, in particular, recognized the strategic importance of this southern outpost, leading to its development as a military and economic center.

The Morne Fortuné, a hill overlooking Vieux Fort, is a significant historical site that provides insight into the town's colonial past. Fortifications on the Morne Fortuné date back to the 17th century and were strategically positioned to protect the southern coast from potential threats. Today, visitors can explore these well-preserved remnants, offering panoramic views of the surrounding landscapes.

In the 19th century, the town of Vieux Fort experienced economic growth with the development of the sugar and cotton industries. Plantations dotted the surrounding countryside, and the town served as a hub for the export of these commodities. The economic activities of this period had a lasting impact on the town's cultural diversity, as laborers from various parts of the Caribbean, including Trinidad and Barbados, were brought to work on the plantations.

The transition from an agrarian economy to a more diversified one in the 20th century brought significant changes to Vieux Fort. The town became a center for commerce and industry, and its proximity to Hewanorra International Airport made it a strategic location for travelers arriving on the island.

Hewanorra International Airport, located near Vieux Fort, has played a crucial role in the development of St. Lucia's tourism industry. The airport, with its modern facilities, welcomes international flights, making it a primary gateway for tourists arriving on the island. This accessibility has spurred the growth of the hospitality sector in Vieux Fort, with numerous hotels and resorts catering to visitors seeking sun, sea, and relaxation.

Vieux Fort's stunning beaches, such as Sandy Beach and Maria Islands Nature Reserve, have become popular destinations for sunbathing and water sports. The nearby Maria Islands, a protected nature reserve, is home to unique flora and fauna and offers opportunities for eco-tourism and nature exploration.

As the southernmost town on the island, Vieux Fort has a unique cultural flavor influenced by its history and the diversity of its residents. The town is known for its vibrant Creole culture, and visitors can experience this through local cuisine, music, and festivals.

One of the notable events in Vieux Fort is the annual Saint Lucia Jazz Festival, which attracts both local and international talent and showcases the island's rich musical heritage. The town's bustling marketplaces offer a taste of St. Lucian life, where fresh produce, spices, and crafts are readily available.

Vieux Fort's role as the "Gateway to the South" extends beyond its economic and transportation significance. It embodies the resilience and adaptability of St. Lucia as it has evolved from a colonial outpost to a vibrant and multicultural town. Today, Vieux Fort welcomes travelers from around the world and invites them to explore the southern wonders of St. Lucia, from its historical sites to its stunning natural beauty, making it an essential stop for those seeking to uncover the soul of the island.

Historical Plantations and Estates

The history of St. Lucia is intricately tied to the plantation economy that flourished during the colonial era. The fertile soils and tropical climate of the island made it an ideal location for the cultivation of cash crops such as sugarcane, cocoa, coffee, and spices. This chapter delves into the legacy of historical plantations and estates that played a pivotal role in shaping the island's past.

One of the most iconic plantations on the island is the Fond Doux Estate, which dates back to the 18th century. This estate, located near Soufrière, offers a window into St. Lucia's colonial history. With its well-preserved buildings and lush landscapes, Fond Doux paints a vivid picture of life on a Caribbean plantation. Visitors can explore the estate's cocoa fields, where the island's famous cocoa beans were once cultivated and processed.

Just a short distance from Fond Doux, the Diamond Estate showcases the remnants of an era when sugarcane was king. This plantation, like many others on the island, played a crucial role in the sugar industry, which was a significant driver of the local economy. The Diamond Estate includes a museum that provides insights into the history of sugarcane cultivation and processing in St. Lucia.

The Balenbouche Estate, located in the southern part of the island, is another historical gem. This estate, which spans over 70 acres, represents a microcosm of St. Lucia's agricultural history. It was once a sugarcane plantation but later diversified its crops to include coconuts, limes, and other tropical fruits. Today, it serves as a working farm, eco-lodge, and heritage site, offering visitors a glimpse into the island's agrarian past. Anse Mamin, an estate near Soufrière, has a unique history. It was originally a sugarcane plantation but was abandoned in the 19th century. In recent decades, it has been revitalized as part of the Anse Chastanet Resort, preserving the estate's historical charm while providing a luxurious escape for modern travelers. The estate's lush surroundings and pristine beaches make it a popular destination for tourists.

The Marquis Estate, situated in the picturesque Roseau Valley, offers visitors a chance to step back in time and explore the island's cocoa and coffee heritage. The estate's fertile lands produce high-quality cocoa beans, and guided tours provide an educational experience about the cultivation and processing of cocoa, an industry that continues to thrive on the island.

La Sikwi Sugar Mill, nestled in the heart of the island, is a testament to the significance of sugarcane in St. Lucia's history. The well-preserved mill, with its massive stone walls and machinery, stands as a reminder of the labor-intensive process of turning sugarcane into sugar. It's a site that allows visitors to appreciate the ingenuity and industry that once characterized these plantations.

St. Lucia's historical plantations and estates, though rooted in a complex history of colonialism and exploitation, represent an important part of the island's cultural heritage. Today, many of these sites have been repurposed for tourism, education, and the preservation of traditional farming practices. They serve as a link between the island's past and present, inviting visitors to explore the agricultural and historical legacies of St. Lucia, while also celebrating its natural beauty and vibrant culture.

Folklore and Legends of St. Lucia

The folklore and legends of St. Lucia are deeply woven into the cultural fabric of the island, reflecting the rich tapestry of its history, traditions, and beliefs. These stories, passed down through generations, offer glimpses into the supernatural, the heroic, and the moral, providing insights into the values and aspirations of the St. Lucian people.

One of the most prominent figures in St. Lucian folklore is the Soucouyant. This malevolent creature, often portrayed as an old woman, is believed to shed her human skin at night to become a fiery ball of light that roams the countryside. She is known for sucking the blood of her victims, often leaving them in a trance-like state. Folklore suggests that protection from the Soucouyant can be found by spreading rice or sand at her doorstep, causing her to count the grains until sunrise, preventing her from returning to her human form.

The La Diablesse, or "Devil Woman," is another well-known character in St. Lucian folklore. She is often depicted as a beautiful woman who conceals her disfigured face. She lures unsuspecting men into the forests, only to lead them astray and vanish. Her appearance is said to be a consequence of a pact with the devil, and it serves as a cautionary tale about the consequences of making deals with dark forces.

In contrast to these malevolent figures, St. Lucia also has its own legendary heroes. One such hero is Charlot, a cunning and fearless individual who outwitted supernatural creatures and villains. His adventures are recounted in various folktales, emphasizing wit and resourcefulness as admirable qualities.

The story of the Jumbie Bird, a mythical creature that appears as a beautiful woman with wings, is another cherished legend. According to folklore, the Jumbie Bird would seduce fishermen and lead them to their doom. The tale carries a moral lesson about the dangers of temptation and the perils of the unknown.

St. Lucia's folklore is also interwoven with stories of Anancy, the trickster spider character prevalent in Caribbean culture. Anancy tales are known for their humorous and clever narratives, often highlighting the triumph of cunning over brute strength.

The island's cultural diversity is reflected in its folklore as well. The Kalinago, the indigenous people of St. Lucia, have their own set of legends and myths. These stories are a testament to their connection with the natural world and their reverence for the spirits that inhabit it.

The legend of Grand Bois, a mystical forest filled with supernatural beings, is cherished among the Kalinago. It is believed to be the dwelling place of ancient spirits and deities, underscoring the spiritual significance of the natural world in their culture.

One cannot discuss St. Lucian folklore without mentioning the annual La Rose and La Marguerite festivals. These celebrations, rooted in both African and French traditions, feature performances, songs, and dances that pay homage to the island's cultural heritage. The festivals center around the rivalry between the La Rose and La Marguerite societies, with each group celebrating its own set of folklore, legends, and ancestral spirits.

The folklore and legends of St. Lucia continue to be an integral part of the island's identity. They are more than just stories; they are a reflection of the collective consciousness, values, and wisdom of the St. Lucian people. These tales have been passed down through generations, enriching the cultural heritage of the island and providing a unique lens through which to view its history and traditions.

Religious and Spiritual Traditions

St. Lucia's religious and spiritual traditions reflect the island's diverse cultural heritage, a tapestry woven with threads of indigenous beliefs, Christianity, and African spirituality. These traditions play a pivotal role in the daily lives and cultural expressions of the St. Lucian people.

Christianity, primarily in its Roman Catholic and Protestant denominations, is the dominant religion in St. Lucia. The influence of Christianity can be traced back to the colonial era when European powers, particularly the French and the British, introduced Christianity to the indigenous population. The Catholic Church played a significant role in shaping the island's spiritual landscape and left a lasting mark on its culture. The majority of St. Lucians identify as Christians, and churches are central to community life, offering not only places of worship but also serving as hubs for social gatherings and events.

The annual Feast of La Rose and the Feast of La Marguerite are two of the most prominent religious and cultural celebrations on the island. These festivals blend Christian traditions with indigenous elements and serve as a unique expression of St. Lucian identity. The Feast of La Rose is associated with the Roman Catholic Church, while the Feast of La Marguerite is linked to the Methodist Church. Both feature vibrant processions, songs, dances, and the crowning of queens.

Beyond Christianity, St. Lucia is also home to a diverse range of spiritual practices and beliefs rooted in African traditions. Obeah, a form of folk magic and spiritualism, is practiced by some St. Lucians. Obeah encompasses a wide spectrum of beliefs and practices, often involving the use of herbs, charms, and rituals to address various concerns, from health and protection to matters of the heart.

The Rastafarian movement has also found a following in St. Lucia, with adherents embracing the spiritual teachings of Haile Selassie, the former Emperor of Ethiopia. Rastafarianism promotes a deep connection to Africa, Afrocentric identity, and a rejection of colonial and Eurocentric values. Reggae music, with its messages of unity, social justice, and spirituality, is an integral part of the Rastafarian culture in St. Lucia.

The island's indigenous Kalinago population, while significantly reduced in numbers due to European colonization, continues to practice their traditional spiritual beliefs and rituals. These include reverence for nature, the use of herbal remedies, and ceremonies to honor ancestral spirits and deities. The Kalinago maintain a strong connection to the natural world, considering it sacred and integral to their way of life.

St. Lucia's spiritual traditions are not limited to formal religions or belief systems. The island's landscape is dotted with sacred sites, from lush rainforests and volcanic peaks to secluded beaches and serene waterfalls. Many St. Lucians hold a deep reverence for the natural world and its spiritual significance. This connection to the land is often expressed through rituals, ceremonies, and the preservation of traditional knowledge about the environment.

In recent years, wellness and holistic practices have gained popularity in St. Lucia, drawing on both traditional and contemporary influences. Yoga retreats, meditation centers, and spas offer visitors and locals opportunities for spiritual and physical rejuvenation amidst the island's breathtaking natural beauty.

In conclusion, St. Lucia's religious and spiritual traditions are a vibrant reflection of its history, cultural diversity, and deep connection to the natural world. Whether through Christianity, African spirituality, or indigenous beliefs, these traditions continue to shape the lives and identities of the St. Lucian people, fostering a sense of community, heritage, and spirituality that enriches the island's cultural landscape.

Art and Music: The Creative Soul of St. Lucia

Art and music are the vibrant threads that weave together the cultural tapestry of St. Lucia, infusing life on the island with color, rhythm, and soul. From the rhythmic beats of soca and calypso to the expressive strokes of local artists, creativity thrives in every corner of this enchanting Caribbean nation.

St. Lucia's musical heritage is deeply rooted in African, European, and indigenous influences, resulting in a diverse and dynamic soundscape. The island is renowned for its contribution to the genres of calypso and soca, with a rich tradition of calypsonians and soca artists who have made their mark on the regional and international stage.

Calypso, with its witty and often socially-conscious lyrics, has been a vehicle for storytelling and social commentary in St. Lucia for generations. Artists like The Mighty Sparrow and The Mighty Gabby have inspired local calypsonians to craft songs that speak to the joys and challenges of everyday life.

Soca, the high-energy offspring of calypso, has a special place in the hearts of St. Lucians, especially during the annual carnival celebrations. Soca rhythms, infectious melodies, and colorful costumes take center stage as revelers move to the pulsating beats of local and regional soca stars.

Traditional folk music also thrives in St. Lucia, with the sounds of bamboo and steel pan bands resonating through the villages during special occasions and festivities. These traditional music forms connect St. Lucians to their African and Caribbean roots, bridging the gap between past and present.

The island's musical talents extend beyond the stage, with many St. Lucians skilled in crafting musical instruments. The creation of drums, flutes, and stringed instruments is a revered craft, passed down through generations. These instruments not only produce enchanting melodies but also serve as symbols of cultural heritage.

Visual arts also flourish in St. Lucia, with local artists drawing inspiration from the island's natural beauty and diverse cultural influences. The works of painters, sculptors, and artisans can be found in galleries and craft markets across the island. Themes of lush landscapes, vibrant street scenes, and expressions of spirituality are common in St. Lucian art.

The Eudovic Art Studio, founded by the renowned artist Vincent Joseph Eudovic, is a beacon of artistic expression in St. Lucia. The studio showcases the intricate art of wood carving, a tradition that has been a part of the island's culture for centuries. Vincent Eudovic's sculptures, inspired by the forms and movements of the human body, exemplify the fusion of tradition and innovation in St. Lucian art.

Carnival, one of the island's most exuberant celebrations, serves as a canvas for artistic expression in various forms. From the elaborate costumes of masqueraders to the dazzling displays of choreographed dance troupes, St.

Lucia's carnival is a vibrant spectacle that merges music, dance, and visual arts.

In recent years, St. Lucia has also embraced contemporary art forms, with local artists exploring new mediums and pushing creative boundaries. The annual Saint Lucia Art Biennial provides a platform for emerging artists to showcase their talents and engage in dialogues about the intersection of art and society.

Art and music education in St. Lucia are vital in nurturing the next generation of creative talents. Schools and cultural institutions offer programs that not only preserve traditional forms but also encourage innovation and experimentation. Young artists and musicians in St. Lucia are inspired by the rich legacy of their predecessors while charting new paths in the world of creative expression.

In conclusion, the art and music of St. Lucia are not just forms of entertainment; they are the lifeblood of the island's culture, connecting generations and preserving the stories, rhythms, and colors of a diverse and dynamic nation. From the spirited beats of soca to the mesmerizing strokes of a painter's brush, the creative soul of St. Lucia continues to flourish, celebrating the island's rich heritage and inspiring future generations to explore the boundless possibilities of artistic expression.

Education and Literacy

Education has been a cornerstone of progress and development in St. Lucia, empowering generations with knowledge and skills to navigate the challenges of an ever-evolving world. The island's commitment to education has paved the way for literacy, innovation, and social advancement, shaping the lives of its citizens and contributing to its overall growth.

St. Lucia's education system is a testament to its dedication to fostering academic excellence and intellectual growth. The island follows a structure that aligns with international standards, comprising early childhood education, primary education, secondary education, and tertiary education.

Early childhood education provides a strong foundation for children, emphasizing the importance of early learning and cognitive development. Primary education is compulsory for children between the ages of five and twelve, ensuring access to basic literacy and numeracy skills. Secondary education follows, catering to students aged thirteen to eighteen, where they prepare for the Caribbean Secondary Education Certificate (CSEC) examinations.

The educational landscape in St. Lucia also includes a wide range of private and parochial schools that offer diverse curricula. These institutions complement the public education system, providing options for families seeking specialized education.

St. Lucia's commitment to education extends to the establishment of the Sir Arthur Lewis Community College, a leading tertiary institution that offers a wide range of programs, including vocational courses and degree programs. The college plays a pivotal role in preparing students for higher education and equipping them with the skills needed to succeed in various fields.

The island is also home to the University of the West Indies (UWI) Open Campus, where students can pursue undergraduate and postgraduate degrees. This affiliation with UWI allows St. Lucians to access higher education without leaving the island, promoting accessibility and affordability.

Literacy rates in St. Lucia have steadily increased over the years, reflecting the success of the education system. According to data from UNESCO, St. Lucia's adult literacy rate stood at approximately 90 percent in recent years, highlighting the nation's dedication to eradicating illiteracy.

Efforts to promote literacy extend beyond formal education. The island's public libraries play a crucial role in promoting reading and literacy among citizens of all ages. These libraries offer a wide selection of books, educational resources, and programs that encourage a love for reading and learning.

Furthermore, the National Youth Council of St. Lucia has launched initiatives to promote literacy and reading comprehension among young people. These programs include book clubs, reading challenges, and outreach efforts to engage the youth in literature and critical thinking.

St. Lucia's commitment to education and literacy has not only empowered its citizens but has also contributed to the island's overall development. An educated workforce has driven economic growth, innovation, and social progress. Moreover, education has been instrumental in fostering a sense of national identity and pride among St. Lucians.

In conclusion, education and literacy are vital pillars of St. Lucia's development and progress. The nation's dedication to providing quality education at all levels, from early childhood to tertiary, has empowered generations with knowledge and skills, ensuring a brighter future for the island and its people. As St. Lucia continues to invest in education, it lays the foundation for continued growth, innovation, and prosperity.

Challenges and Triumphs of St. Lucia

St. Lucia, like many nations, has faced its share of challenges throughout its history. From colonial oppression to economic struggles, the island has navigated turbulent waters. Yet, it is also a place of resilience, determination, and triumph. This chapter delves into the challenges that have shaped St. Lucia and the triumphs that have emerged from adversity.

Colonialism cast a long shadow over St. Lucia, with both the French and the British vying for control over the island. This rivalry subjected the indigenous Kalinago people to displacement and oppression. The island changed hands several times between the 17th and 18th centuries, as it swung back and forth between French and British control. These colonial struggles left an indelible mark on St. Lucia's history and culture.

The era of sugar, slavery, and plantations brought profound suffering to St. Lucia's population. Enslaved Africans endured harsh labor conditions and cruelty. The legacy of slavery, with its profound social and economic consequences, continued to shape the island's society long after emancipation in 1834.

Economic challenges persisted in the post-slavery era. The collapse of the sugar industry in the late 19th century left many St. Lucians struggling to find alternative livelihoods. Agriculture, particularly the cultivation of bananas, emerged as a key economic driver in the early 20th century.

World War I and World War II had their impacts on St. Lucia, with the island contributing troops and resources to the war efforts. These global conflicts disrupted trade and had economic repercussions.

The road to independence was marked by political and social struggles. St. Lucia gained self-government in 1967 and achieved full independence from British rule in 1979. The journey towards independence was not without its challenges, but it marked a significant triumph for the nation.

In more recent times, the island has faced economic challenges, including vulnerability to natural disasters such as hurricanes. Despite these difficulties, St. Lucia has sought to diversify its economy, focusing on tourism as a key industry. The island's breathtaking landscapes, cultural richness, and warm hospitality have made it a sought-after tourist destination.

Environmental challenges, including issues related to deforestation and coral reef degradation, have prompted conservation efforts. St. Lucia is committed to preserving its natural beauty, recognizing that its ecosystem is vital for both tourism and the well-being of its citizens.

The nation has made significant strides in healthcare and education, with a growing emphasis on public health and literacy. St. Lucia's educational system is highly regarded in the region, and the island's healthcare infrastructure continues to improve.

Cultural preservation has been a triumph in its own right. St. Lucia's folk traditions, music, and festivals remain vibrant, showcasing the resilience of its cultural heritage.

In conclusion, St. Lucia's history is a testament to the challenges it has faced and the triumphs it has achieved. From the scars of colonialism and slavery to the path to independence and economic diversification, the island's story is one of perseverance and resilience. St. Lucia continues to navigate the complexities of the modern world while celebrating its rich cultural heritage and natural beauty, exemplifying the spirit of triumph in the face of adversity.

St. Lucia's Role in the Caribbean Community

St. Lucia, nestled in the heart of the Caribbean, plays a significant role in the Caribbean Community (CARICOM), a regional organization aimed at fostering economic integration, political cooperation, and social development among its member states. St. Lucia's participation in CARICOM reflects its commitment to regional unity, economic growth, and collaboration on critical issues affecting the Caribbean region.

CARICOM, founded in 1973, brings together 15 member states and 5 associate members, creating a platform for dialogue, cooperation, and collective action. St. Lucia is one of the original member states, illustrating its early commitment to regional integration.

One of the primary objectives of CARICOM is to promote economic development and cooperation among its member states. St. Lucia, like many of its Caribbean neighbors, faces economic challenges, including vulnerability to external shocks, limited resources, and the need for diversification. Through CARICOM, St. Lucia has access to regional resources, technical assistance, and collaborative initiatives designed to bolster economic growth.

Trade is a vital component of CARICOM's agenda, and St. Lucia benefits from the Common External Tariff (CET), which facilitates intra-regional trade by harmonizing customs duties on imports from outside the Caribbean region. This promotes trade among member states, creating economic opportunities for St. Lucian businesses and fostering economic resilience.

CARICOM has also been instrumental in advocating for the interests of its member states on the global stage. St. Lucia, like its counterparts, relies on the collective strength of the organization to address critical issues such as climate change, economic vulnerabilities, and access to international financing. CARICOM's unified voice amplifies the concerns and priorities of its member states in international forums.

The organization plays a pivotal role in advancing regional security and stability. The Caribbean Community implements initiatives to combat transnational crime, drug trafficking, and other security challenges. St. Lucia benefits from these efforts, contributing to the safety and security of its citizens and visitors.

St. Lucia's participation in CARICOM is not limited to economic and political collaboration; it extends to cultural and social exchange. The organization supports cultural preservation and celebrates the rich tapestry of Caribbean heritage. St. Lucia, with its vibrant cultural traditions and festivals, contributes to this cultural mosaic.

Furthermore, CARICOM fosters educational and human resource development through initiatives like the Caribbean Examinations Council (CXC) and the University of the West Indies (UWI). St. Lucian students have access to educational opportunities within the region, enriching the nation's human capital.

CARICOM's response to health crises, such as the HIV/AIDS epidemic and more recently, the COVID-19 pandemic, underscores its commitment to the well-being of the Caribbean people. St. Lucia, like other member states, benefits from collaborative efforts in healthcare and disease prevention.

In conclusion, St. Lucia's role in CARICOM is emblematic of its commitment to regional integration, economic development, and cooperation on shared challenges. As a member state, St. Lucia leverages the collective strength of the organization to address economic, social, and political issues while celebrating the rich cultural diversity of the Caribbean. Through CARICOM, St. Lucia stands united with its Caribbean neighbors, working towards a brighter and more resilient future for the entire region.

Tourism's Impact on St. Lucia's Economy

Tourism is the lifeblood of St. Lucia's economy, driving economic growth, providing employment opportunities, and contributing significantly to the nation's overall prosperity. The island's breathtaking landscapes, rich cultural heritage, and warm hospitality have made it a sought-after destination for travelers from around the world. This chapter explores the profound impact of tourism on St. Lucia's economic landscape.

Tourism in St. Lucia has a long history, dating back to the early 20th century when visitors were drawn to the island's natural beauty and therapeutic mineral springs. However, it was in the latter half of the 20th century that tourism experienced significant growth, becoming a key pillar of the nation's economy.

St. Lucia's appeal lies in its diverse range of attractions. The iconic Pitons, a pair of towering volcanic peaks, are UNESCO World Heritage Sites and symbols of the island's unique natural beauty. Lush rainforests, pristine beaches, and coral reefs teeming with marine life add to the island's allure.

The tourism sector encompasses various segments, including luxury resorts, boutique hotels, eco-tourism ventures, and cruise tourism. This diversity ensures that St. Lucia caters to a wide range of visitors, from honeymooners seeking romantic getaways to adventurers looking for eco-friendly experiences.

Cruise tourism plays a vital role in St. Lucia's tourism industry. The island welcomes hundreds of thousands of cruise ship passengers annually, who explore its attractions, shop for local crafts, and contribute to the local economy.

The tourism sector has a significant multiplier effect on the St. Lucian economy. It drives demand for a wide array of goods and services, from agriculture and fisheries to the creative arts and cultural experiences. Local artisans and craft producers benefit from the sale of handmade souvenirs and artworks.

One of the most significant contributions of tourism to St. Lucia's economy is employment. The sector employs a substantial portion of the island's workforce, providing jobs in hospitality, transportation, tour operations, and other related fields. It also creates opportunities for entrepreneurship, as locals establish businesses to meet the needs of tourists.

The revenue generated by tourism is a crucial source of foreign exchange earnings for St. Lucia. It supports infrastructure development, the preservation of natural and cultural assets, and investments in healthcare and education.

To sustain and enhance its tourism industry, St. Lucia has adopted responsible and sustainable practices. The island places a strong emphasis on preserving its natural environment and cultural heritage, ensuring that future generations can enjoy the same pristine landscapes and traditions that draw visitors today.

In recent years, St. Lucia has also explored niche tourism markets, such as wellness and adventure tourism. These initiatives attract travelers seeking unique and transformative experiences.

The government of St. Lucia, in collaboration with private sector partners, continually invests in tourism infrastructure, including airport facilities and accommodations, to ensure the island's competitiveness in the global tourism market.

While tourism has brought significant economic benefits to St. Lucia, it also poses challenges, including environmental sustainability and the need for infrastructure development to accommodate growing numbers of visitors. These challenges require careful planning and management.

In conclusion, tourism is the engine that drives St. Lucia's economy, offering employment, generating revenue, and promoting the nation's natural and cultural treasures to the world. With a commitment to sustainable practices and ongoing investment, St. Lucia's tourism industry continues to flourish, contributing to the nation's overall development and prosperity.

Environmental Conservation Efforts

Environmental conservation is a pressing concern in St. Lucia, a nation blessed with stunning natural beauty and unique ecosystems. The island's commitment to preserving its environment is evident in the various initiatives and policies aimed at safeguarding its fragile ecosystems, mitigating climate change impacts, and fostering sustainable development.

One of the central pillars of St. Lucia's environmental conservation efforts is the protection of its marine resources. The island's coral reefs are vital to both the marine ecosystem and the tourism industry. Recognizing this, St. Lucia has established marine protected areas (MPAs) to safeguard coral reefs, seagrass beds, and other critical habitats. These MPAs promote sustainable fishing practices and limit harmful activities that can degrade marine ecosystems.

Land-based conservation is equally essential. St. Lucia boasts lush rainforests and unique flora and fauna. The St. Lucia Forestry Department oversees efforts to protect and manage these natural resources. Reforestation programs, along with strict regulations on logging and land use, aim to maintain the integrity of the island's forests.

The endemic species of St. Lucia, such as the St. Lucia parrot (Amazona versicolor), are integral to the island's biodiversity. Conservation programs work tirelessly to protect and recover these species from the brink of extinction. These efforts involve habitat restoration and captive breeding programs.

Climate change poses a significant threat to St. Lucia, with rising sea levels, extreme weather events, and changing precipitation patterns affecting the island. The government, in partnership with international organizations, has implemented climate resilience and adaptation strategies. These include disaster risk reduction measures, sustainable land management practices, and the development of climate-resilient infrastructure.

Sustainable agriculture practices are crucial for reducing environmental impacts. St. Lucia promotes organic farming, agroforestry, and responsible land use to minimize soil erosion and chemical runoff. These practices not only protect the environment but also ensure food security for the nation.

Waste management is another vital aspect of environmental conservation. St. Lucia has made strides in waste reduction, recycling, and proper disposal. Public awareness campaigns encourage responsible waste management, reducing the burden on landfills and minimizing pollution.

Efforts to conserve energy and reduce carbon emissions are evident in St. Lucia's transition to renewable energy sources. Solar and wind energy projects have been introduced to reduce dependence on fossil fuels and lower greenhouse gas emissions.

St. Lucia is a signatory to international agreements and conventions related to environmental conservation, including the Convention on Biological Diversity and the United Nations Framework Convention on Climate Change. These commitments reinforce the nation's dedication to global efforts to protect the environment.

Educational initiatives and community engagement are essential components of St. Lucia's environmental conservation efforts. Schools, organizations, and local communities participate in environmental awareness campaigns, tree planting, and beach cleanups, instilling a sense of responsibility for the environment among citizens.

In conclusion, St. Lucia's commitment to environmental conservation reflects the island's recognition of the profound importance of its natural heritage. The nation's efforts encompass marine and terrestrial conservation, climate resilience, sustainable agriculture, waste management, and renewable energy adoption. Through these initiatives, St. Lucia strives to preserve its environment for future generations while contributing to global efforts to combat climate change and protect biodiversity.

Resilience and Recovery: Natural Disasters

St. Lucia's idyllic landscapes and tropical climate come with a price—the island is vulnerable to a range of natural disasters, including hurricanes, floods, landslides, and volcanic activity. Throughout its history, St. Lucia has faced these challenges with resilience and determination, focusing on recovery and disaster preparedness to protect its citizens and safeguard its future.

Hurricanes are among the most significant natural threats to the island. Located in the hurricane-prone Atlantic Basin, St. Lucia is susceptible to these powerful storms, which can bring devastating winds, heavy rainfall, and storm surges. The impact of hurricanes on the island's infrastructure, agriculture, and coastal communities can be severe.

To mitigate the effects of hurricanes, St. Lucia has developed robust disaster preparedness and response mechanisms. The National Emergency Management Organization (NEMO) plays a central role in coordinating disaster management efforts. Early warning systems, including meteorological alerts and evacuation plans, help protect lives and minimize damage.

Flooding is another common consequence of heavy rainfall associated with hurricanes and tropical storms. Low-lying areas and riverbanks are particularly vulnerable. St. Lucia has invested in flood mitigation measures, including river dredging and the construction of retaining walls to reduce the risk of flooding.

Landslides pose a threat, especially in the mountainous regions of St. Lucia. Heavy rainfall can trigger landslides, endangering homes and transportation routes. The government conducts geological surveys to identify high-risk areas and takes measures to stabilize slopes and protect communities.

Volcanic activity is a unique threat to St. Lucia, primarily centered around the Sulphur Springs area in Soufrière. While the island's volcano, the Soufrière Volcano, has been dormant for many years, monitoring systems are in place to detect any signs of potential eruptions. Public education campaigns inform residents and visitors about safety measures in case of volcanic activity.

Seismic activity also affects St. Lucia due to its location near tectonic plate boundaries. Earthquakes, though relatively rare, can occur. Building codes and infrastructure standards incorporate seismic resilience measures to minimize damage during earthquakes.

Post-disaster recovery efforts in St. Lucia are comprehensive and involve government agencies, international organizations, and local communities. These efforts encompass restoring essential services, rebuilding infrastructure, and providing assistance to affected individuals and businesses.

International assistance and cooperation play a vital role in disaster recovery. St. Lucia benefits from regional organizations such as the Caribbean Disaster Emergency Management Agency (CDEMA) and international aid agencies that provide support in the aftermath of disasters.

Efforts to enhance resilience extend to climate change adaptation strategies. St. Lucia recognizes the long-term impacts of climate change on sea-level rise and extreme weather events. The nation is committed to reducing greenhouse gas emissions and implementing sustainable land-use practices to protect its future.

Community involvement and public awareness campaigns are integral to building resilience. St. Lucians are encouraged to be proactive in disaster preparedness, from creating emergency kits to participating in evacuation drills.

In conclusion, St. Lucia's vulnerability to natural disasters has necessitated a proactive approach to resilience and recovery. The nation's commitment to disaster preparedness, early warning systems, and sustainable practices reflects its determination to protect its citizens and preserve its natural beauty. St. Lucia's experience serves as a valuable lesson in the importance of resilience in the face of nature's formidable forces.

St. Lucia's Future: Aspirations and Challenges

St. Lucia stands at a pivotal juncture in its history, with a future filled with both aspirations and challenges. As the nation looks ahead, it does so with a steadfast commitment to building a more prosperous, sustainable, and inclusive future for its citizens and generations to come.

One of the key aspirations for St. Lucia's future is continued economic growth and diversification. While tourism remains the cornerstone of the island's economy, the government recognizes the importance of reducing dependence on a single sector. Efforts are underway to promote investment in other areas, such as agriculture, manufacturing, and renewable energy. These initiatives aim to create jobs, increase resilience to external shocks, and ensure a more balanced economy.

Environmental sustainability is a paramount concern for St. Lucia's future. The island's natural beauty is its greatest asset, and preserving it is crucial. St. Lucia has embraced initiatives to protect its coral reefs, forests, and biodiversity, understanding that a healthy environment is essential for tourism and the well-being of its citizens. Climate change adaptation and mitigation strategies will continue to be at the forefront of the nation's agenda.

Education and human resource development are central to St. Lucia's aspirations. The island places a high value on its citizens' education and seeks to provide quality learning opportunities. Investments in early childhood education, vocational training, and tertiary education contribute to a skilled and competitive workforce.

Healthcare remains a priority, with efforts to improve access to quality medical services and promote public health initiatives. A robust healthcare system is essential for the well-being of St. Lucians and the sustainability of the tourism industry.

Infrastructure development is a critical aspect of St. Lucia's future plans. Investments in transportation, including road networks and airport facilities, are aimed at improving connectivity and accessibility. Modernizing infrastructure not only benefits residents but also enhances the island's appeal to tourists and investors.

St. Lucia's future also envisions social inclusivity and equity. Initiatives to reduce poverty, address inequality, and empower marginalized communities are ongoing. The nation recognizes that progress should benefit all its citizens, regardless of their background or circumstances.

Global partnerships and cooperation are integral to St. Lucia's future. The island actively participates in regional and international organizations, fostering diplomatic relations and promoting its interests on the global stage. Collaboration with neighboring Caribbean nations and engagement with international institutions are vital for addressing common challenges.

While St. Lucia aspires to a bright future, it faces several challenges. Economic vulnerabilities, including exposure to external shocks and the need for job creation, remain pressing concerns. Climate change poses threats to the island's environment and economy, requiring ongoing adaptation efforts. Healthcare and education systems require continuous improvement to meet evolving needs.

Social challenges, such as reducing crime rates and addressing substance abuse, require a multifaceted approach. Balancing development with environmental preservation is a constant struggle, as the island strives to ensure economic growth does not come at the cost of its natural beauty.

In conclusion, St. Lucia's future is shaped by a vision of sustainable development, environmental stewardship, social equity, and economic diversification. While challenges are present, the nation's determination, resilience, and commitment to its people and environment bode well for a future that holds the promise of continued progress and prosperity. St. Lucia stands ready to embrace the opportunities and confront the challenges that lie ahead on its journey toward a better tomorrow.

Conclusion

In tracing the rich tapestry of St. Lucia's history, from its ancient roots to its vibrant present, and envisioning its future aspirations and challenges, we embark on a journey that reveals the essence of this Caribbean gem. St. Lucia, a nation nestled in the heart of the Lesser Antilles, boasts not only breathtaking landscapes but also a captivating history, a resilient spirit, and a commitment to progress.

The ancient roots of St. Lucia, with traces of indigenous peoples dating back centuries, lay the foundation for a diverse and culturally vibrant nation. The influences of Amerindian, African, European, and East Indian heritage converge to create a harmonious blend of traditions, customs, and beliefs that define St. Lucia's cultural identity.

Early European exploration and colonization left an indelible mark on St. Lucia, as it became a prized possession in the rivalry between the French and the British. The island changed hands multiple times, each colonial era shaping its landscape and culture.

The legacy of sugar, slavery, and plantations, a painful chapter in St. Lucia's history, is a testament to the resilience of its people. The struggle for freedom and the eventual emancipation of enslaved individuals marked a turning point, laying the foundation for a more equitable society.

Colonial St. Lucia, often a battleground for European powers, witnessed a complex interplay of politics and rivalries. Its strategic location in the Caribbean made it a coveted prize, with military conflicts leaving their mark on the island.

The rise of the banana industry in the 20th century transformed St. Lucia's agricultural landscape. This shift from sugar to bananas heralded a new economic era, bringing economic opportunities to rural communities.

World Wars and St. Lucia's contributions to the global conflicts underscored the island's commitment to international solidarity. The sacrifices made during these tumultuous times are remembered with gratitude.

The road to independence in 1979 marked a significant milestone, granting St. Lucia the autonomy to shape its destiny. The nation took its place among the family of nations, forging its path to self-determination.

Modern politics and governance have seen St. Lucia embrace democratic principles and institutions. The nation's leaders navigate the challenges of governance while striving for development and prosperity.

Cultural diversity and heritage form the soul of St. Lucia, with vibrant traditions, festivals, and artistic expressions that celebrate its unique identity.

The flora and fauna of St. Lucia, from its lush rainforests to its coral reefs, are treasures to protect and preserve. Environmental conservation efforts ensure that future generations can cherish the island's natural beauty.

Culinary traditions and delicacies reflect St. Lucia's multicultural influences, with a rich tapestry of flavors that tantalize the taste buds.

Iconic landmarks like the Pitons and Sulphur Springs are testaments to St. Lucia's geological wonders, drawing visitors from across the globe.

Historical gems like Pigeon Island and bustling hubs like Rodney Bay tell the stories of a nation with a storied past and a vibrant present.

As we contemplate St. Lucia's role in the Caribbean community, we see a nation that actively participates in regional initiatives, promoting cooperation and unity among its neighbors.

Tourism's impact on St. Lucia's economy is undeniable, driving growth, creating employment, and showcasing the island's natural beauty to the world.

Environmental conservation efforts underscore the nation's commitment to protecting its ecosystems and safeguarding its future.

Resilience in the face of natural disasters is a hallmark of St. Lucia's spirit, as the island prepares for and recovers from hurricanes, floods, and other challenges.

Looking ahead, St. Lucia's aspirations include economic diversification, environmental sustainability, education, healthcare, and social inclusivity.

Challenges, from economic vulnerabilities to climate change, will require ongoing dedication and innovation to overcome.

In conclusion, St. Lucia's history, culture, and future aspirations are a testament to the resilience, determination, and spirit of its people. This Caribbean jewel continues to shine brightly on the global stage, inviting visitors to explore its beauty and welcoming its citizens to shape a future filled with promise. St. Lucia's story is one of hope, progress, and the enduring spirit of a nation with a bright future ahead.

Thank you for taking the time to read this book on the fascinating history, culture, and future of St. Lucia. We hope you found it informative and engaging, providing you with valuable insights into this beautiful Caribbean nation.

If you enjoyed reading this book and found it valuable, we kindly ask for your support in the form of a positive review. Your feedback is invaluable to us, as it helps us continue to create content that informs, educates, and entertains our readers.

Please consider leaving a review to share your thoughts, whether it's about the content, writing style, or any other aspect of the book. Your reviews not only motivate us but also assist other potential readers in making informed decisions about their reading choices.

Once again, thank you for your time and interest in our work. We sincerely appreciate your support, and we look forward to hearing your thoughts through your review.

Printed in Great Britain
by Amazon